2nd Edition

61 Gems on Highway 61

Your Guide to
MINNESOTA'S NORTH SHORE
From Well-Known Attractions to Best-Kept Secrets

by Kitty Mayo and William Mayo

Adventure Publications
Cambridge, Minnesota

Acknowledgments

We want to acknowledge our families, as always, as the source of meaning for our lives in this world. We are so grateful for the goodness we receive from those who love us no matter what. That kind of debt can never be truly repaid. The best we can do here is remember those dear to us and pass this hope and love on to our children. All of our relatives are here in our words, in our attempt at communicating the beauty of this place we love, the North Shore of Lake Superior.

All photos by William Mayo except front cover and pg. 7, used under license from Shutterstock.com

Cover and book design by Jonathan Norberg

Edited by Brett Ortler

10 9 8 7 6 5 4
61 Gems on Highway 61: Your Guide to Minnesota's North Shore
First Edition 2009
Second Revised Edition 2018
Copyright © 2009 and 2018 by Kitty Mayo and William Mayo
Published by Adventure Publications
An imprint of AdventureKEEN
310 Garfield Street South
Cambridge, Minnesota 55008
(800) 678-7006
www.adventurepublications.net
All rights reserved
Printed in China
ISBN 978-1-59193-794-4 (pbk.); ISBN 978-1-59193-795-1 (ebook)

61
Gems
on *Highway* 61

MINNESOTA
61

Table of Contents

Gooseberry Falls (see pg. 48)

About Highway 61

Minnesota State Highway 61 runs
south-north from Duluth, Minnesota,
all the way to the Canadian border.
Our 61 gems occur along the highway,
and we've given you directions to get
from Highway 61 to each site. For the
purpose of clarity, we're assuming
you're heading north from Duluth
("up" the shore). Each gem is num-
bered sequentially from Duluth; the
higher the number, the farther away it
is from Duluth. If you're coming from
the north, that's no problem—simply
note that lower-numbered gems are
farther south (and closer to Duluth).

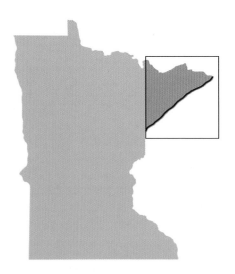

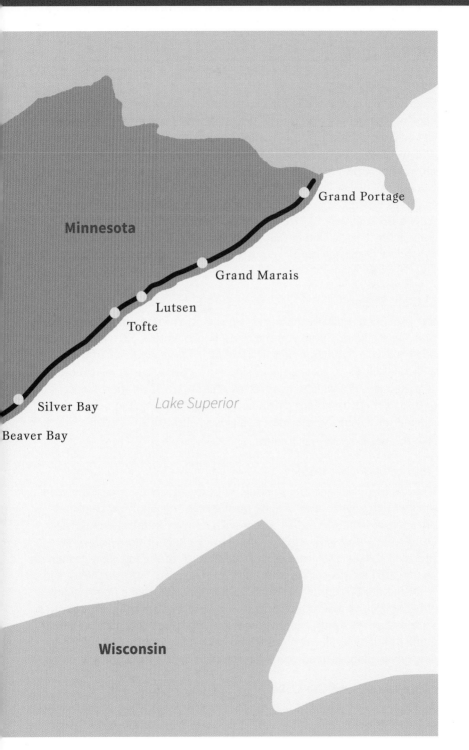

Grand Portage

Minnesota

Grand Marais

Lutsen

Tofte

Silver Bay

Lake Superior

Beaver Bay

Wisconsin

Introduction

About This Book

Highway 61 is renowned for its cliffside views of the lake, the many nearby state parks, and tourist destinations like Two Harbors and Grand Marais. But there's even more here than that—in fact, there are dozens of wonderful sites hidden along Highway 61 that are beautiful, interesting, and worthwhile. These are the true gems of Highway 61, fascinating places that are unknown even to many locals. We've spent our lives visiting and cataloging these special places, and during our travels on Highway 61, we have often wondered, "Where did that name come from?" or "What is that place about?" We wrote this book to try to answer these questions and to share our insider's knowledge with you, in order to show you a side of Highway 61 most people rarely see.

Classic Sites

But some of the well-known sites on the north shore are just too good to pass up, so we're giving you the best of both worlds. We've designated some places as "classic" sites, (five in all). These are some of the most well-known places on the north shore; everyone should visit these sites at least once. We've labeled these as "classic sites" on their respective pages, so check them out. Even better, combine a visit to one of the lesser-known sites with a visit to a classic site—this way you'll see the best the north shore has to offer.

How to Use This Book

Duluth, Minnesota, is the starting point for this book. All of the sites follow Highway 61, and the site numbers in this book are based on distances north of Duluth—a gem with a lower number is closer to Duluth than one with a higher number. To help orient you, we've included the distance (in miles) from Duluth in the top right corner. Of course, this means we're assuming you're driving "up" the north shore (heading north), but if you're doing the opposite, that's no problem either. If you're driving south, a lower gem number simply means that a site is farther south. Finally, we want you to use this book as a field guide to Highway 61, as a quick and easy reference for the ride. But don't over-plan; instead, see what happens as the road unfolds.

Highway 61 and the Lake

As Highway 61 winds along, the sheer cliffs provide breathtaking views of Lake Superior, mile after mile. Epitomized on Bob Dylan's "Highway

61 Revisited," this famous road once ran from New Orleans through Duluth and to the Canadian border. Though Highway 61 is included in many blues ballads, Dylan wrote a different kind of tribute, one that flowed from the northern reaches of his birthplace, showing the world that the blues highway went both ways.

Lake Superior

Lake Superior is the largest of the five Great Lakes and the greatest of the Great Lakes. It holds 10 percent of the Earth's freshwater and it is the largest freshwater lake in the world (by surface area). The power and fury of the Lake rivals any body of water; her strength and unpredictability have demanded the respect of mariners for thousands of years. Melville even acknowledges this in *Moby Dick: Those grand fresh-water seas of ours . . . are swept by Borean and dismasting blasts as direful as any that lash the salted wave. They know what shipwrecks are, for out of sight of land, however inland, they have drowned full many a midnight ship with all its shrieking crew.*

The Power of the Lake

It goes almost without saying—the Lake's dramatic cliffs, not to mention its riptides and undertows, can be humbling and even dangerous. Then again, this specter of danger is part of what intrigues us, what makes us sit up and pay attention. The Lake is also a simple joy; many family picnics, marriage proposals, weddings, and honeymoon trips have taken place here, making the Lake a treasure enjoyed for generations.

Take it From Us

Here are some words of advice from two veterans. Remember to bring along extra clothes, a pair of dry socks, and extra shoes in case the Lake sneaks up on you as you walk along. And always bring an extra jacket or flannel shirt. You are likely to find out that the weather along the Lake can change radically in a very short amount of time. You should expect cooler weather than what the forecast says, or what the temperature appears to be when you leave your hotel. It is often 10 to 20 degrees colder by the Lake, and a strong wind off of the water can make it feel even brisker. Be prepared for all types of weather, including fog. And bring warm clothes; you won't have fun if you are cold!

Please also bear in mind that the Lake is as dangerous as it is beautiful; the Lake is powerful and unforgiving. As much as we find kinship with her, we are ever called to pay respect to her power. Slippery rocks, ledges, and cliffs should be traversed with caution and we beg you—keep children under your close supervision. Too often we have observed visiting folks who were unaware of the perils at hand let their progeny skip along too close to danger; we want everyone to be safe. Streams and rivers might look appealing on a hot day, but unless you are familiar with the vagaries of a particular waterway, you should stay out and enjoy it from the shore. The Lake herself can have an undertow strong enough to pull an adult swimmer out to sea, and it should not be trifled with if you are uncertain of conditions.

Caution—Wildlife

Driving on Highway 61 should not be taken lightly either; please use caution and pay close attention to the changing conditions along the road. Deer are an ever-present danger and the best advice we can give you is to watch for them, drive a reasonable speed, and DO NOT SWERVE! Swerving cars are liable to end up in the ditch, or worse, running into oncoming traffic. So counsel yourself against swerving. Remind yourself ahead of time because it is instinctive. As terrible as it is to think of hitting the animal directly, the consequences of swerving could make matters much, much worse. If impact appears unavoidable, slow as quickly as you SAFELY can (do not slam on the brakes or you will lose control) and, keeping control of the vehicle, get to the side of the road, out of the path of traffic. If the animal is still on the road, call 911 so that it can be moved.

Driving on Highway 61—Passing and Pullouts

Another word about safe driving—there are many pullouts onto the highway that are hard to see, so pay attention as you pull out and be aware of traffic coming from both directions. We strongly advise against passing on Highway 61, even where it is legal. Try to sit back and relax. You are on vacation and the ride is half the fun. It's better to get there safe than fast. If the car in front of you is going slower than the speed limit, the passengers are probably just enjoying the view. And it's not a bad idea to slow down because the wonderful views often give way to sheer cliffs and twists and turns; this is not a place you want your vehicle to leave the road!

Getting Oriented

While driving can be a little dicey, it's difficult to get lost on Highway 61, as the road simply goes north-south from Duluth to Canada. For the purpose of clarity, this book is about Minnesota State Highway 61.

For consistency's sake, we measured all sites from the same point in Duluth where Highway 35 turns into London Road/MN Highway 61 (at 26th Avenue East).

Minnesota Highway 61 vs. Old Highway 61

Nevertheless, a few of the sites near Duluth are a bit trickier to find. Here, another highway, St. Louis County Road 61 (known as Old 61), parallels Minnesota 61. Almost all of the sites in this book occur on Minnesota State Highway 61, but three sites (the Old Pump House at Lakewood, Stoney Point, and the Buchanan Settlement Marker, Gems 3, 4, and 5) are actually on Old Highway 61. We recommend you start in Duluth,; visit the first two sites; jump onto Old 61 for sites 3, 4, and 5; and then follow Old 61 until just before Two Harbors, where it merges with MN-61. After that, all sites in the book are right off of Minnesota Highway 61.

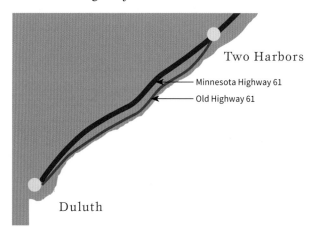

Have Fun!

After all those dire warnings, please be assured that spending time here with your friends, lover, or family will always be rewarding, as long as you are aware of your surroundings, and the potential risks, and you are prepared. We hope that our insiders' point of view helps you make wonderful memories, and we hope others come here who will do their best to take care of the Lake too. We recognize the spirit of adventure and exploring that will drive you to look for more treasures; it has driven us. And we know the Lake's tranquility can be a balm for a busy life, for there is nothing better than being lakeside. Welcome to the most beautiful place on Earth!

.5 mile from Duluth

1
EXIT HERE

Glensheen Mansion
Duluth

Two Harbors

Beaver Bay

Silver Bay

Gem 1

CLASSIC SITE

Glensheen Mansion

How to Get There: As you are leaving Duluth and heading north on London Road, which will turn into Highway 61, the mansion will be on your right. It is well marked. Turn right into the large parking lot just past the main building off of London Road.

Accessibility: The main tour is conducted on the lower level and first floor of the mansion; they are wheelchair accessible.

Cool Things to Know: No true collection of North Shore icons would be complete without mentioning the mysterious and magnificent Glensheen Mansion. Chester Congdon set out to create a mansion worthy of the ages and reflective of his status as a captain of industry. His home seems Gothic and castle-like today. Money, Victorian opulence, and murder make this storied place definitely worth checking out. Although it is not spoken of openly by today's caretakers (who are employees of the University of Minnesota campus in Duluth), everyone knows what happened here—a notorious murder. Even if you never take the tour or go beyond a glimpse as you drive by on London Road headed for Highway 61, a peek is all it takes to look backward in time. Stately doors and windows wrapped in stone and protected by a massive wrought iron fence seem to speak of feudal lords and past centuries. Yet, despite all its grandeur, when you step through the doors of the Congdon castle, it is somehow warm and welcoming. Maybe it's just an illusion, but it feels like home. You will probably have the same impulse to call out, "Honey, I'm home!" when you step into the warm, wood-paneled entry, interspersed with intricate

Tofte Lutsen Grand Marais Grand Portage

engravings. Don't miss your chance to visit the impressive and brooding Glensheen Estate—no trip to the North Shore would be complete without it.

Stately doors and windows wrapped in stone and protected by a massive wrought iron fence seem to speak of feudal lords and past centuries.

Gem 2

Brighton Beach (Kitchi-Gammi Park)

How to Get There: Just past the sky blue Visitor Center shack and after the Lester River, look for a large brown sign that reads "Kitchi-Gammi Park," then turn right onto a mile-long paved road (Brighton Beach Rd.) with many pullouts and parking spaces. This will eventually lead to Old Highway 61, also known as St. Louis County Highway 61/Congdon Boulevard. Follow Old 61 to Gems 3, 4, and 5; Old 61 joins MN-61 just before Two Harbors.

Accessibility: Parts of this area are not wheelchair accessible, but the view from the car is worthwhile and most should be able to access the picnic area and benches.

Cool Things to Know: Known to us locals as Brighton Beach, the official signage reads "Kitchi-Gammi Park." Whatever name you use, you will have a pleasant visit. An uncommonly cool spot during summer months, you might find some visitors enjoying the natural air-conditioning. In addition to the barbecue areas, beach, and lava flows to explore, you might notice migrating birds passing by. Many picnic tables and benches throughout the area make for a splendid setting for an impromptu meal. "Bella's Castle," another mysterious name, is a small, sturdy WPA (Works Progress Administration) pavilion that may save your repast from the temperamental lake-effect weather. Visitors may be tempted to test the waters here, but be aware of the life-threatening undertow. Enjoy the view, though. This is a great place to watch ships moving to and from the twin ports

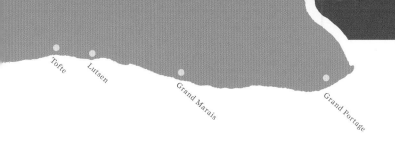

of Duluth and Superior. Try to notice the difference between the "Salties," or ocean-going vessels, and "Lakers," the cargo vessels that traverse only the Great Lakes. While you watch, you can learn a little nautical lingo by calling which way the ships are traveling. Although it may seem counterintuitive, boats headed into port here are said to be "up bound," while those leaving and heading to the Sault Ste. Marie locks are "down bound."

Bella's Castle is a WPA-era pavilion at Brighton Beach.

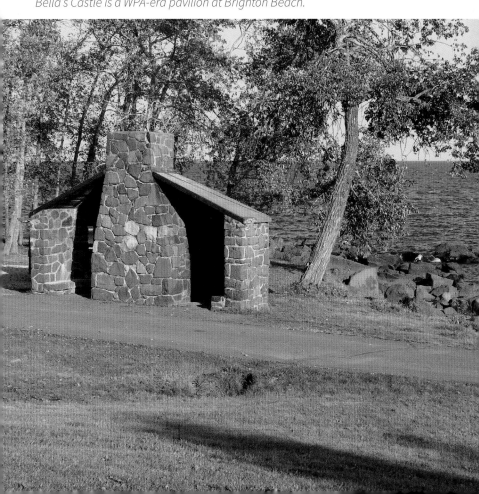

5 miles from Duluth

3
EXIT HERE

Old Pump House
at Lakewood

Duluth

Two Harbors

Beaver Bay

Silver Bay

Gem 3

The Old Pump House at Lakewood

How to Get There: Just past the turn-off for Brighton Beach Road, 3 miles north of Duluth, turn right onto County Road 61 (also known as Old 61 or Congdon Boulevard). Continue 2 miles. The Pump House will be on your right. Follow Old 61 to Gems 4 and 5; Old 61 rejoins MN-61 just outside of Two Harbors. The site's address is 8131 Congdon Boulevard.

Accessibility: It's easy to take pictures from the roadside.

Cool Things to Know: Here you will find a grand building. Known officially as the Duluth Water Pumping Station, its architecture is more reminiscent of a castle or a fortress. Still in service, the structure was built in 1897 and was powered by steam-driven pumps until 1932. The station provides all the water for the entire city of Duluth, as well as for Proctor, Hermantown, and Rice Lake Township. The system is old; many of the pipes have been in the ground for 120 years and some of the reservoirs are from the 1880s. If you could see inside, you would find the original hand-operated bridge crane. There is a spigot near the parking area where you are welcome to help yourself and fill your water bottles with free, cold, filtered water, fresh from Lake Superior! The water you drink can only be had from local taps; thus far, attempts to bottle and sell Lake Superior's water have been resisted. This is also a good place to access the shore for a short break. On the little beach below the Pump House, you will be at the spot where the 500-foot steamer *Crescent City* ran up on the rocks during the

Tofte
Lutsen
Grand Marais
Grand Portage

Mataafa Storm of November 1905. The storm led to many shipwrecks and lives lost, though the *Crescent City* was laboriously salvaged.

Known officially as the Duluth Water Pumping Station, its architecture is more reminiscent of a castle or a fortress.

14.5 miles from Duluth

4
EXIT HERE

Stoney Point

Duluth

Stoney Point

Two Harbors

Beaver Bay

Silver Bay

Gem 4

Stoney Point

How to Get There: On Old 61, travel about 8 miles from the Old Pump House at Lakewood. Turn right off of Old 61 onto Stoney Point Drive. This gravel road travels about 1 mile before rejoining Highway 61. There are numerous spots where there is enough room on the shoulder to park safely.

From Highway 61 Expressway, head north of Duluth for about 10 miles. Turn right at Alseth Road and follow it for about 1 mile all the way to Stoney Point Drive.

Accessibility: This is a great place to view the lake, and because it's so accessible by car, anyone can pull off to the side of the road and get an eyeful without even getting out. The road also offers a nice place to take a stroll to stretch your legs, and it is relatively even and flat. Getting down to the water's edge requires some scrambling on rocks, so use caution.

Cool Things to Know: Well known by locals as a great place to head to when the weather is roaring out of the northeast, this is an ideal spot for watching the Lake in her wild moods. When waves are crashing in a good blow, the spray can sometimes fly up over the road, giving you a safe front-row seat to the Lake at her most tempestuous.

The lay of the land, angle of the shore, and power of Lake Superior make this a favorite spot of surfers who say it rivals some of the best surfing locales in the world. A good day for surfing can happen even in mid-winter, and, if you are lucky, you'll see many brave souls riding the waves here in full wetsuits. In good weather, you can explore the expanse of black basalt lava flow that is marked by clear striations and gouges left behind by the glaciers about 12,000 years ago.

Stoney Point is the perfect place to introduce visitors to the never-ending blue of the Big Lake.

15 miles from Duluth

5
EXIT HERE

Duluth

Buchanan Settlement Marker

Two Harbors

Beaver Bay

Silver Bay

Gem 5

Buchanan Settlement Marker

How to Get There: About 9 miles past the Old Pump House (Gem 3) and just past where Stoney Point Drive rejoins Old 61, you'll find the pullout on the lakeside, 1.25 miles south of the Knife River. Look for a sign that reads "Historical Site." To rejoin MN-61, follow Old 61 north; the two roads merge just before Two Harbors.

Accessibility: There are steps leading down to the plaque area, and it is wheelchair accessible.

Cool Things to Know: A strange sense of what might have been lingers at this deteriorating, yet lovely, historical site. A stone marker rises grandly, made more stately by the small plaza that reminds us that this was once the seat of the United States Land Office of the northeast district. From 1856 to 1859, the founders of Buchanan (named after the then U.S. President) had high hopes of creating a boomtown, as they believed that there was lots of copper in the nearby bed of the Knife River. With nearly endless white pine forest all around, fur-bearing animals of all kinds, and access to the ports of Duluth and Superior, everything seemed to be in place. Before all these dreams were dashed, Buchanan became a town of firsts: It was home to the first post office on the North Shore and the first North Shore newspaper (the *North Shore Advocate*, published 1857–1858). Unfortunately, the copper failed to pan out and plans fell apart. Shortly thereafter, the land office moved to Duluth. With no reason to exist, the town was quickly abandoned; later, the empty buildings were destroyed by forest fire. Today it is hard to visualize where a hotel, several saloons, boarding houses, a steam dock, a post office, and a newspaper building would have been. But they were all there. Properly speaking, it could be called a ghost town, but Buchanan is a city of the past, where not even the ghosts remain.

Properly speaking, it could be called a ghost town, but Buchanan is a city of the past and completely empty; not even the ghosts remain.

22 miles from Duluth

6
EXIT HERE

Duluth

Two Harbors
Pierre The Voyageur

Beaver Bay

Silver Bay

Gem 6

Pierre The Voyageur

How to Get There: From Duluth, follow Highway 61 north for 22 miles until you arrive at the outskirts of Two Harbors, just past the tiny town of Larsmont. Watch for Pierre just past the car dealership. Turn right onto Stanley Road from Highway 61 (or left onto Stanley if you've been traveling on County 61/Old 61), and then turn into the parking lot adjacent to the statue. Pierre is located next to the Earthwood Inn Bar and Grill.

Accessibility: The Earthwood Inn welcomes visitors who want to get a close-up view or take a photo with our voyageur friend. (Pierre even has his own Facebook page.) The parking lot is gravel, and there are some minor inclines between the lot and the statue of Pierre.

Cool Things to Know: Built in 1960 within Two Harbors proper, Pierre stood guard at the center of the complex that included a museum, since vanished, and a motel that is still operating. Back then, he was a well-known attraction, and he greeted visitors in his booming voice. But he eventually became the subject of a property issue (the land Pierre was situated on was sold), and he was eventually moved to a new location. In 2011, Pierre was reborn. First, he made a 1.5-mile journey to the edge of town, where he was given a new home at the Earthwood Inn. Then he received a much-needed face-lift. The complete overhaul included beautification, fresh paint, and a new paddle, as well as fake boulders to stand on and a birchbark canoe at his side. Better yet, if you press a button, Pierre now can even "speak" for a minute or two.

Enthusiasts of roadside sculptures like Pierre consider such monuments to be examples of Americana architecture.

Pierre is even considered a historical landmark by prestigious institutions such as the Smithsonian Institution and the University of Minnesota.

With a new home and new life, Pierre's feeling great. There's no mistaking a twinkle in his eye, so be sure to wave!

A monument to fun, Pierre was placed on the Smithsonian's list of historic landmarks.

22 miles from Duluth

7
EXIT HERE

Beaver Bay

Silver Bay

Duluth

The Tugboat Edna G.
Two Harbors

Gem 7

The Tugboat *Edna G.*

How to Get There: From Highway 61 in Two Harbors, turn right onto Waterfront Drive/6th Street. Waterfront Drive crosses the train tracks and then bends to the right. Follow that to a parking lot where there is a viewing platform for the tug. You will be able to walk down from there, or drive a bit farther to a dirt track leading right up to the dock.

Accessibility: You can drive right up to the dock, but the boat itself isn't wheelchair accessible.

Cool Things to Know: In 1896, the president of the Duluth & Iron Range Railroad named his company's new tugboat after his daughter, Edna Greatsinger. Today the *Edna G.* is not only regarded as an icon of the North Shore and Two Harbors, Minnesota, but it was placed on the National Register of Historic Places in 1974. These days she is idled and permanently docked next to the ore docks in the town she served admirably for so many years. In her time, she held many roles: as an ordinary tug for the massive ore carriers in Agate Bay, as an icebreaker, a fireboat, and as a vessel involved in many rescues on the open lake. Her retirement is well earned, though she still stands ready for those with an interest to come aboard and pay her a visit.

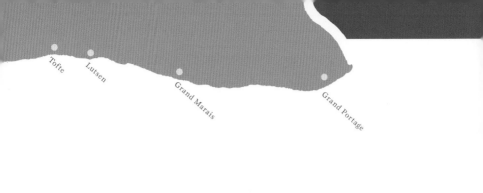

Tofte

Lutsen

Grand Marais

Grand Portage

After a century, she's still a fine-looking vessel.

22 miles from Duluth

8
EXIT HERE

Duluth

The Three-Spot Train Engine
Two Harbors

Beaver Bay

Silver Bay

Gem 8

The *Three-Spot* Train Engine

How to Get There: In Two Harbors, turn right off of Highway 61 onto Waterfront Drive/6th Street. Follow Waterfront Drive toward the Lake for 7 blocks. At that point you will have reached the edge of town, and you'll see the train depot on your left. The engine will be right next to it.

Accessibility: The engine is located just off the parking lot, and the area is wheelchair accessible.

Cool Things to Know: Covered with a protective canopy, old Engine #3, later nicknamed the *Three-Spot*, rests comfortably. This noble chunk of iron and steel holds a very special place in the history of the North Shore and Minnesota. She was transported in 1883 by rail from Philadelphia to Duluth. As no rail line existed at that time between Duluth and Two Harbors, the last leg of her voyage was completed by boat. Chained down on a stout barge, she was tugged to Agate Bay in Two Harbors with the help of the worthy tug *Ella G. Stone*. Halfway there, a sudden northeasterly gale blew up, threatening to capsize the barge. At one point the captain told his crew to stand by with axes should it become necessary to cut away the cable that held the barge to the tug; burdened as it was, the tremendous weight of the engine would no doubt have pulled the tug down as well. Fortunately, through skillful seamanship and steady nerves, the *Ella G.* and her captain arrived at Agate Bay with the engine safely in tow. There the *Three-Spot* began a long and distinguished career. As it hauled the first load of iron ore dug out of the ground of the Iron Range, she was lauded and given great respect. Today the old *Three-Spot* appears as ready as ever to perform her duties.

Tofte Lutsen Grand Marais Grand Portage

You are free to walk right up and lay your hands upon this piece of American history. And right next door there's even more fun—a much larger engine and the Lake County Historical Society Depot are just nearby.

Today the old Three-Spot *appears as ready as ever to perform her duties. You are free to walk right up and lay your hands upon this piece of American history.*

9
EXIT HERE

Duluth

Two Harbors

Two Harbors Lighthouse
Bed and Breakfast Inn

Beaver Bay

Silver Bay

Gem 9

Two Harbors Lighthouse Bed and Breakfast Inn

How to Get There: In Two Harbors, turn right off of Highway 61 onto Waterfront Drive/6th Street. Follow the brown signs directing you to the breakwall at Agate Bay. Once in sight of the water, you'll notice the lighthouse. Follow the narrow dirt driveway to the garage behind the lighthouse. Reservations can be made online through the Lake County Historical Society (www.lighthousebb.org).

Accessibility: The inn is not wheelchair accessible.

Cool Things to Know: Imagine yourself back in time, 100 years ago, sleeping under the sweeping light of this beacon, in the very bedroom where the chief keeper of the light slept. During the week, you might climb the stairs of the tower to be sure that all was well at sea. If you could do this today, would you? Well, you can! The Two Harbors Lighthouse Inn is open year-round, and you could be one of the few people who can say they've spent a night in a working lighthouse. Guests have the opportunity to explore the rich history of the lighthouse firsthand, with a private look into its inner workings. Here you can spend an evening in the sitting room with a keen eye towards the weather and watch over the harbor with a guardian's care. Because of the elevation and the view, the weather and sky are more intense, but this sturdy brick house is reassuringly cozy. And the area around the lighthouse is full of wildlife, a strange juxtaposition to the industry of the working harbor. In the morning you can look forward to a sumptuous

Tofte

Lutsen

Grand Marais

Grand Portage

breakfast served by Lake County Historical Society staff who are knowledgeable about the area and happy to suggest places for you to explore. If you are unable to stay the night, stop for a self-guided tour of the grounds and exhibits. If you do that, chances are you will want to make plans to stay here!

The Two Harbors Lighthouse Bed and Breakfast Inn is open year-round, and you could be one of the few people who can say they've spent a night in a working lighthouse.

Duluth

Two Harbors
Two Harbors Breakwall

Beaver Bay

Silver Bay

Gem 10

Two Harbors Breakwall

How to Get There: In Two Harbors, turn right off of Highway 61 onto Waterfront Drive/6th Street. Follow the brown signs directing you to the breakwall at Agate Bay. The breakwall is situated on Agate Bay next to the lighthouse. Even better, the Lighthouse Point trail entrance is here too!

Accessibility: There is a wheelchair ramp leading down to the breakwall. The breakwall itself is flat, wide, and easily wheelchair accessible.

Cool Things to Know: First called *Wass-we-wining*, or "Place to Spear Fish by Torchlight," by Native Americans, the first European settlers set up shop right here in 1856. At the end of the long parking area you will see the impressive cement wall, girded with boulders, reaching like an arm across the mouth of Agate Bay. One half of Two Harbors (Burlington Bay is the other), Agate Bay's harbor is home to the industries that put the town on the map—the lumber and pulpwood industry, commercial fishing, and the iron ore industry, which has been the biggest overall influence on the area. Iron ore was first transported here by train in 1884. As you walk the wall you will notice Dock #1, closest to the tugboat dock, which, at the time of its construction, was the largest iron ore loading dock in the world. There were once six loading docks here, all built of wood. Smaller docks were also present and were meant for goods and passengers, and the shore bristled with the shacks and docks of the local fishermen.

The breakwall itself was developed in stages and extends about a third of a mile into the wide water. About 100 years

Tofte

Lutsen

Grand Marais

Grand Portage

ago, when it was not connected to shore and was not as large, the lighthouse keeper had to row out to the end to fuel the oil lamp there. Walk on the breakwall in any weather and you will be close to where the sky and water converge.

The Two Harbors Breakwall is an impressive cement wall, girded with boulders, reaching like an arm across the mouth of Agate Bay.

22 miles from Duluth

11
EXIT HERE

Sonju Trail
Two Harbors

Duluth

Beaver Bay

Silver Bay

Gem 11

Sonju Trail

How to Get There: In Two Harbors, turn right off of Highway 61 onto Waterfront Drive/6th Street. Follow the brown signs directing you to the breakwall at Agate Bay. Once you find the breakwall parking lot, just look to your left. At the end of the lot you will spot an arched passageway; this is the trail's starting point. The lighthouse bed-and-breakfast is right nearby too!

Accessibility: The trail at Burlington Bay end is paved; the rest of the trail is moderately difficult.

Cool Things to Know: With little fanfare other than a sculpted arch marking its beginning, you will find this trail to be a hidden treasure that allows you to stretch your legs and meander along the prettiest point in Two Harbors. The path is paved and winds along the rocky coast, through majestic cedar stands and past masses of raspberry brambles. You might pause at one of the scattered benches to watch the waves break against the shore, or perhaps you would like to leave the path and cast about amid the ancient lava flows. Either way, you will get the sense of being in a wild area preserved within a stone's throw of the active ore docks and boat launch. The many deer you might spot are not very wary and are used to being fed by guests staying at the Lighthouse Bed and Breakfast. This wild point also hosts fox, rabbits, and a variety of squirrels, with the occasional black bear, lynx, or moose passing through. We hope that the threat of development continues to be staved off so that we all can enjoy the presence of so much natural beauty so close to town. This miniature ecosystem is unique in its diversity and it supports a host of creatures and plants; nevertheless, it is sensitive to human influence.

Stretch your legs and meander along the prettiest point in Two Harbors.

22 miles from Duluth

12
EXIT HERE

Beaver Bay

Silver Bay

Trail of Whispering
Giants Sculpture
Two Harbors

Duluth

Gem 12

Trail of Whispering Giants Sculpture

How to Get There: Proceed all the way through Two Harbors on Highway 61 (7th Avenue) just to the edge of town. Turn right into the Visitor Center. You will find the sculpture at the edge of the parking lot.

Accessibility: The area is easy for all to access.

Cool Things to Know: American sculptor Peter Wolf Toth presented this impressive work to the people of Minnesota out of respect and regard for its original inhabitants and their plight. Originally created and erected in 1977, the statue was refurbished 31 years later, when the artist returned after hearing from concerned citizens that his creation was falling into disrepair. Unpaid and virtually unnoticed, he set up camp next to his monument, and over the course of a few weeks he began the arduous task of restoring and preserving the 30-foot sculpture. Now catalogued by the Smithsonian, it and 70 others are regarded as important works of American art. Without ceremony, Mr. Toth left Two Harbors, and he left the fruits of his labor behind for the American people. With gratitude, we would like to acknowledge this fine work that everyone can enjoy. Toth spent 1972 to 1988 traveling the U.S., donating his time, labor, and creative energy, carving a Native American monument in each state. He completed a total of 71 statues, including 12 in various Canadian provinces. This entire "collection" of sculptures has come to be called *The Trail of Whispering Giants*. At the Visitor Center you will also find an original CCC (Civilian

Conservation Corps) cabin filled with maps, brochures, and people of good cheer with good information. They welcome you to use their picnic tables and enjoy their expansive lawn at any time.

American sculptor Peter Wolf Toth presented the impressive work to the people of Minnesota out of respect and regard for its original inhabitants.

22 miles from Duluth

13
EXIT HERE

Duluth

Burlington Bay
Two Harbors

Beaver Bay

Silver Bay

Gem 13

Burlington Bay

How to Get There: Go through the town of Two Harbors and turn right onto Park Road, just past the Visitor Center. Look for the municipal campground signs. In about 200 yards you will see a small parking area on your left.

Accessibility: The area has uneven terrain, but it's easy for most to access. The sandy beach makes this area inaccessible for those in wheelchairs.

Cool Things to Know: One half of Two Harbors (Agate Bay is the other), this bay makes for a nice stop at the water's edge. The tiny town of Burlington stood over this bay for a few years starting in 1856, though it consisted of little more than a steam sawmill and a few shacks. When the bustling pioneer town of Two Harbors came into its own, Burlington Bay was often the site of recreation, boating, fishing, and old-time picnics on the "jumping rocks." If you are ever inclined to swim in the Lake, this would be a good place to do it, with its sandy beach and far-reaching shallow sand bottom. We will warn you that though we have braved the ice-water here, the average temperature is 38 degrees Fahrenheit, with the surface temperature in the summer months sometimes between 40 and 65 degrees Fahrenheit. That may sound warm enough to swim in, but temperatures in the high end are rare and very temporary. Even if the surface is warm, the water just below that is likely 45 degrees, so you are likely in for a very short dip! This is a great place to cool your heels, but it is far more common on a sultry day to see the beach's edge lined with people in swimming attire and not one soul in the Lake. From here, you have easy access to the beautiful

Sonju Trail. This trail gently rises and falls among old white pines and is curiously sheltered and private, considering how close it is to the road. Nearby you will also find the city campgrounds, with sites for tents and RVs.

When the bustling pioneer town of Two Harbors came into its own, Burlington Bay was often the site of recreation.

Gem 14

Flood Bay

How to Get There: About 1 mile north of Two Harbors, on the right. Watch for the blue sign that reads, "Flood Bay Wayside."

Accessibility: All can have a great view from the parking lot, but there are gentle steps down to the beach.

Cool Things to Know: Every North Shore beach has its own character, and each visit is a unique experience. It doesn't matter if the weather is howling and you feel nature's power, or the Lake is sweetly rocking and you feel its peace; every visit at every bit of shore is worthwhile. This is particularly true for Flood Bay, a natural harbor with a panoramic view and a pebble beach. The bay was named for a settler who operated a small steam sawmill here in 1856; the bay was an important log landing and rafting site. Today at Flood Bay, you'll often find piles of driftwood heaped up by a past day's storm, and you'll have the chance to search for treasure among the multitudes of tiny agates, always hoping, of course, for that whopper! To find them, try sitting or lying down right on the stones. As you turn over new layers, scan each square inch slowly. Sometimes your best luck will come when you get down close to the layer of damp stones. Agate hunting is good for the soul. It can slow you down and help relax your breathing, heart rate, and blood pressure as you focus only on finding that whopper. It's a simple pleasure, and even if you don't find any $1 million gems, cherish the journey. Feel close to it all as you listen to the water, feel the shape and weight of each rock in your hand, and discover the joy in such an unhurried, basic pursuit.

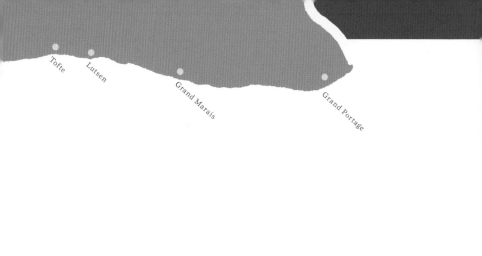

Tofte Lutsen Grand Marais Grand Portage

At Flood Bay, search for treasure among its multitudes of tiny agates.

25 miles from Duluth

15
EXIT HERE

Duluth

Two Harbors

Kelsey Beach

Beaver Bay

Silver Bay

Gem 15

Kelsey Beach

How to Get There: Located 3 miles north of Two Harbors. Immediately after crossing the Stewart River Bridge, turn right into a dirt parking lot. Kelsey Beach is right across the road from Betty's Pies.

Accessibility: There is a somewhat uneven, short path to the beach; it is not wheelchair accessible.

Cool Things to Know: Follow the path northeast on this beach and you'll find something secretive and special, an area claimed by some to have mystical powers. Visit this beach in any kind of weather and you no doubt will begin to feel the ancient peace that is resident here. This small beach of cobblestone extends beyond the small sanctuary to intriguing formations of stilled lava. Different aspects of this sheltered place reveal themselves at different times of day, but its intimate grandeur is unparalleled at dawn. Skip a stone here in the name of a loved one, or see if you can find the place where it appears that a bear's claw marks have been preserved in fossil form. Look for the tiny rivulets that form miniature falls. Try this: Sing something. Together or alone, raise your voice in song and let it join with the great Lake. Offer it up as a shout of joy or a prayer. Something happens here, and it is good. And if that's not enough, visit the nearby Stewart River, which was named for settler John Stewart in 1856 and used for log driving. A logjam once developed near the river's mouth that took three years to clear. You can still see traces of the old splash dams upriver.

Tofte

Lutsen

Grand Marais

Grand Portage

This small beach of cobblestone extends beyond the small sanctuary and features intriguing formations of stilled lava.

Gem 16

Silver Creek Cliff Trail

How to Get There: About 4.5 miles north of Two Harbors, immediately after the Silver Creek Tunnel, pull into the parking lot on your right. You will find the trail running alongside the bluff.

Accessibility: There is a well-paved trail from the parking lot.

Cool Things to Know: At 398 feet, Silver Creek Cliff is the highest bluff rising directly out of Lake Superior. Early roads ran inland, but in 1923, blasting created a dramatic and death-defying road that hugged the outer edge of the cliff. For those of us who remember it, it was the most hair-raising part of an already challenging drive, with plummeting heights and deer herds that seemed to love congregating in the middle of the road. But despite the danger, it was also one of the most gorgeous drives in the country. Since then, this sheer drop-off was converted to a bike and walking trail. Today, the main highway cuts through the cliff itself. The current road is about 125 feet above the Lake; when you pass through the tunnel, which was finished in 1998, picture the remaining 273 feet of rock suspended above your head. According to local lore, a family of feral goats once lived atop the bluff back in the '30s, and when a few local residents spotted a young goat in distress on an outcrop, they mounted a rescue to reunite it with its mother. While the cliff may not soar to the heights it used to, every time you pull over here you will be entranced by the grand view. This is one of those rare places that gives that strange feeling that you are standing inside of a postcard, so have your camera ready and record this stunning vista.

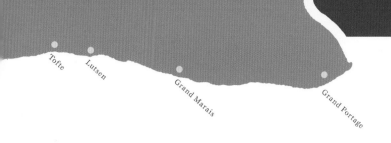

Tofte   Lutsen

Grand Marais

Grand Portage

And if you want a good hike, a Gitchi-Gami State Trail trailhead is nearby as well (see pg. 54).

This sheer drop-off was converted to a bike and walking trail. Today, the main highway cuts through the cliff itself.

32 miles from Duluth

17
EXIT HERE

Duluth

Two Harbors

Wolf Rock of the
Superior Hiking Trail

Beaver Bay

Silver Bay

Gem 17

Wolf Rock of the Superior Hiking Trail

How to Get There: Wolf Rock is 10 miles north of Two Harbors. To get there, take a left off of Highway 61 onto Lake County 106, travel 2.3 miles on that dirt road until you find the (marked) Superior Hiking Trail parking lot on your right. On the right (east) side of the parking lot, there is a sweet little path leading up a steep incline but for less than a half mile. The Superior Hiking Trail office is located in Two Harbors, but the official start of the trail is located near Jay Cooke State Park.

Accessibility: The trail is steep and not for everyone; it's short and not wheelchair accessible.

Cool Things to Know: The Superior Hiking Trail is a largely unheralded gem of the North Shore and is one of the most comprehensive trail systems in the whole country. Offering mile after mile of unparalleled vistas, it follows the ridgeline above the Lake, starting south of Duluth and ending near the Canadian border, spanning roughly 310 miles. The beauty of this phenomenal trail is that it provides an endless amount of recreational opportunities. You can take a short hike, enjoy day trips, or make a commitment to living on a wilderness trail, as campsites and primitive shelters are available along the way. There are many ways to approach this trail; you can even arrange for a service to pick you up at the end of your hike and transport you into the lap of accommodation luxury. But if you want a shorter foray, follow us to the top of Wolf Rock, which, according to the

Tofte

Lutsen

Grand Marais

Grand Portage

Superior Hiking Trail office, is "one of the best spots for a quick fix of the trail." Rising steadily from the parking lot, it might only take you 10 minutes to discover a stunning, expansive view of the Lake and surrounding countryside that is guaranteed to take your breath away.

The beauty of this phenomenal trail is that it provides an endless amount of opportunities. You can take a short hike, enjoy day trips, or make a commitment to living on a wilderness trail, as campsites and primitive shelters are available along the way.

35 miles from Duluth

18
EXIT HERE

Gooseberry
State Park

Beaver Bay

Silver Bay

Gooseberry Falls

Two Harbors

Duluth

Gem 18

CLASSIC SITE

Gooseberry Falls State Park

How to Get There: On Highway 61, turn right at the brown signs for Gooseberry Falls State Park. You will turn at the first left into the parking lot for the Visitor Center. Located 13 miles north of Two Harbors.

Accessibility: The Visitor Center is wheelchair accessible. There is a long, well-paved path leading down to a view of the waterfalls. The path is gently sloping but includes switchbacks.

Cool Things to Know: If you only have time for one stop on your North Shore drive, make sure it's at Gooseberry Falls State Park. Only 35 miles past Duluth, it has been a favorite destination since the 1920s, when driving the North Shore for kicks began. Since then, Gooseberry has lost none of its allure. With enough to occupy you for a day or a week within the state park's boundaries, you will have access to boundless trails, lava flow formations, lakeshore, and river beaches. Explore the awesome Visitor Center or stay in the campgrounds that border the Lake. There are miles of trails and vista after vista from endless vantage points. Again, if you have time for only one thing in the park, do not miss the main waterfalls. They aren't the biggest or most dramatic waterfalls on the North Shore, but they may well be the easiest to get right up next to. If the water levels are right, you will even be able to meander in the midst of the water as it trails over long rock ledges between falls. The bridge that spans the river as a continuation of Highway 61 is beautiful from below and gives you the opportunity to walk across the river, right beneath the highway.

Tofte
Lutsen
Grand Marais
Grand Portage

*Don't climb wet rocks or let children do so; there are serious injuries in Gooseberry Falls State Park every year. Although there are no fences keeping you out, please exercise good sense in determining safe use of these natural wonders.

If you only have time for one stop on your North Shore drive, make sure it's at Gooseberry Falls State Park.

35 miles from Duluth

19
EXIT HERE

Duluth

Two Harbors

Water Tower at
Gooseberry Falls
State Park

Beaver Bay

Silver Bay

Gem 19

Water Tower at Gooseberry Falls State Park

How to Get There: Just 13 miles north of Two Harbors, turn right at the brown signs for Gooseberry Falls State Park. Once in the park, proceed past the Visitor Center and follow the signs for the Lady Slipper Building. You will see it on your right, about 30 feet from the road.

Accessibility: There is a short dirt path leading up to the tower from the roadway, an easy walk for most. This might be difficult for those in wheelchairs, but it's easy to view from the road.

Cool Things to Know: Encased in red and blue granite, the water tower in Gooseberry State Park looks like something from a fairy tale or a mystery from the past. It houses a 10,000-gallon tank built in 1935 by the CCC (Civilian Conservation Corps) to serve the nearby picnic area. With no well available nearby, workers filled it from the CCC camp well a distance up river (on the other side of the highway bridge). In an uncommon move by a public service agency under severe financial constraints, the CCC program sought to create beautiful structures that blended architecture with natural beauty. In this spirit they hired architect U.W. Hella and two Italian masons to create the tower, which would beautify and cool the water tank. It stands 25 feet tall with a 17-foot diameter. No longer in use, it stands as a testament to what can be accomplished in unity, for the greater good, even in the most difficult of times. The stonework of the CCC buildings in Gooseberry includes some of the most distinctive masonry in all of Minnesota's state parks. Of course, while you are there you should enjoy all that the park has to offer. Above the highway bridge there are two waterfalls with a total drop of 30 feet, and there are two falls below with a total drop of 75 feet. There are more than 10 miles of foot trails, a fifth waterfall upstream, and even an agate beach at the mouth of the river downstream.

The water tower in Gooseberry Falls State Park looks like something out of a fairy tale or a mystery from the past.

Gem 20

Belle P. Cross Anchor, Gooseberry Falls State Park

How to Get There: The *Belle P. Cross* anchor is located in Gooseberry Falls State Park, about 13 miles north of Two Harbors. Turn right at the brown signs to enter the park. Continue through Gooseberry past the water tower until you come to the end of the parking area. Walk past the picnic area toward the shore.

Accessibility: There are a few steps, but overall it's an easy stroll; it's not wheelchair accessible.

Cool Things to Know: Once the site of a major logging operation, the mouth of the Gooseberry River has returned to its natural state and is a lovely place to picnic, stroll, or cast a line. With dramatic cliffs on either side of a large sandbar, you can imagine the urgency you'd feel if you had to contend with the 15-foot rollers while trying to find the safety of shore. That's what the *Belle P. Cross* had to contend with. On April 29, 1903, the ship was driven inland by a snowstorm and sank at the mouth of the Gooseberry River. Remarkably, no lives were lost—the 18 sailors stepped right onto the lumber dock without getting their feet wet! Lumber vessels like the *Belle P. Cross* once towed a record-breaking log raft of 6 million board feet of lumber all the way to Michigan. Making the trip in eight days, the crew brought along carrier pigeons to send for help in case of trouble. We have snorkeled here with the freezing waters of the Lake on one side of the sandbar and the relative bath water of the river on the other side. We found no sunken treasure, but you will find the anchor of this worthy

ship high above the shore nearby. Weighing in at about 1,500 pounds, it has a noteworthy history; it once traveled around Lake County in the back of a pickup driven by five boisterous youngsters. Go ahead and give it a heft. Can you imagine moving that huge chunk of metal with four of your friends?

On April 29, 1903, the Belle P. Cross *was driven inland by a snowstorm and sank at the mouth of the Gooseberry River.*

Gem 21

Gitchi-Gami State Trail

How to Get There: Located just 16 miles from Two Harbors at mile marker 42, the Twin Points Public Water Access is a great place to get to the trail. It is uncrowded, with lots of parking. To get there, just turn right into the lot off of Highway 61.

Accessibility: The trail has outstanding accessibility, with newer pavement and wide pathways.

Cool Things to Know: The Gitchi-Gami State Trail has been in development for years, and the sections completed so far include 29 miles of paved thoroughfare safely away from the cars on Highway 61. The trail was the dream of some forward-thinking individuals, and that dream is coming true one mile at a time. Envisioned by the Gitchi-Gami Trail Association as a safe corridor for bikers, skaters, joggers, and walkers, a dedicated group of volunteers has helped keep this good idea alive for several decades. When the trail is completed, it will stretch 86 miles between Two Harbors and Grand Marais and will connect five state parks, four scientific and natural areas, and several historic sites. It is a good thing to see this kind of tenacity; right now only various segments are completed, but every year more work is finished. The longest section now is between Gooseberry Falls State Park and Beaver Bay. Twin Points is an excellent place to hop on, as the trail connects several communities and gives all of us the opportunity to get closer to it all. Visit the Gitchi-Gami State Trail (www.ggta.org) website for more specifics, as well as the chance to throw a little support their way for all the hard work they are doing on our behalf.

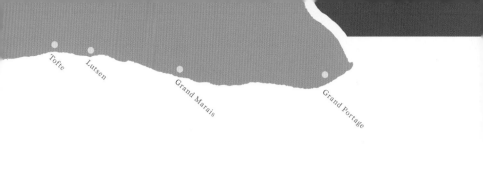

Tofte

Lutsen

Grand Marais

Grand Portage

The Gitchi-Gami State Trail is a safe corridor for biking, skating, jogging, or walking along the North Shore.

Gem 22

Iona's Beach

How to Get There: At mile marker 42 on Highway 61, turn right into the well-marked parking lot. Hike north on the short trail to Iona's Beach Scientific and Natural Area.

Accessibility: The area is not difficult, but it's also not wheelchair accessible.

Cool Things to Know: Located between Gooseberry Falls State Park and Split Rock State Park, Iona's Beach is designated an SNA (Scientific and Natural Area). It is named after Iona Lind, the former owner of Twin Points Resort. Iona and John Lind ran their resort here for 50 years; then the family made it a gift to the public as a preserve. It is managed by the Sugarloaf Association and designated an SNA by the DNR. One of the few beaches of significant size on the Lake, this one begins at a northern shore cliff of pink rhyolite and felsite bedrock, then stretches over 300 yards to another cliff of dark gray basalt. This magical pink beach is known for the tinkling sounds the waves make as the flattened pebbles, or "shingles," settle again; listen closely and you can hear the gentle, clinking sound and feel it through your feet. Whether you walk the whole beach, where dark stones are a rarity, or just stand, look, and listen, you will get a sense of the many families that spent decades returning to this beloved spot year after year.

Tofte

Lutsen

Grand Marais

Grand Portage

This magical pink beach is known for the tinkling sounds the waves make as the flattened pebbles settle.

Duluth

Two Harbors

Split Rock Falls

Beaver Bay

Silver Bay

Gem 23

Split Rock Falls

How to Get There: About 18 miles from Two Harbors, look for mile marker 43 on Highway 61. There you'll see the Split Rock River pullout/parking lot. Park there, and then take the Superior Hiking Trail Split Rock Spur and head away from the lake. As soon as you reach the first branch of the trail, take a right and head into the ravine.

Accessibility: This unpaved path winds down into a fairly steep ravine and is not wheelchair accessible.

Cool Things to Know: This is another genuine gem of the North Shore. Though somewhat diminutive compared to the High Falls or Devil's Kettle, it receives much less foot traffic. This section of the Superior Hiking Trail culminates with a respectable 20-foot waterfall, a lovely wooden bridge, and a little forest canyon, a small universe of its own. After making the half-mile hike at a gradual incline, the main trail continues onward and a small, steep, somewhat narrow path leads you down to the river's edge and a sturdy wooden bridge. To the left, the falls tumble over a gray granite cliff. Trees and shrubs on either side of the falls crown the water and frame the sky. Immediately to your right, just before the bridge, is the perfect place to have a picnic, as an area approximately 20 feet in diameter lies waiting beneath a cluster of mature cedar trees. Here the river curves sharply to the right and is flanked by a large rock outcropping, perhaps 50 or 60 feet high. The river moves gently against the earthen bank on the opposite shore, and couples will find this place enchanting and untrammeled. Save this one for something special.

Tofte Lutsen Grand Marais Grand Portage

On the West Split Rock River you will find a waterfall, a lovely wooden bridge, and a little forest canyon, creating a small universe of its own.

41 miles from Duluth
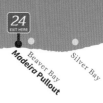

24
EXIT HERE

Duluth

Two Harbors

Madeira Pullout
Beaver Bay

Silver Bay

Gem 24

Madeira **Pullout**

How to Get There: To get to the *Madeira* Pullout, follow Highway 61 to Two Harbors. Then continue for 19 miles and turn right onto an old patch of 61 that forms a horse-shoe off the new section of highway, just past mile marker 45. Within a few feet you can park in a pullout to the right, along a section lined with a renovated stone wall.

Accessibility: The area is accessible for everyone.

Cool Things to Know: This is the perfect place to take great photos of one of the prettiest lighthouses in the country, perched on its cliff over the lake. Here you can take in the only view of Split Rock Lighthouse from a safe pullout on Highway 61. When you do, consider this: When the lighthouse was under construction in 1910, there were no serviceable roads. Everything came by boat and was hauled up the 100-foot sheer cliff. The Mataafa Storm of 1905, which caused the wreck of the *Madeira*, was the final impetus for the construction of Split Rock Lighthouse. (In the storm, 29 ships were lost, along with 215 sailors.) The remains of the *Madeira* lie below the surf, her name emblazoned in yellow lettering still visible on the bow. The *Madeira* struck the sheer cliff of Gold Rock Point broadside, and one Fred Benson scaled the 60-foot cliff to secure a line that saved nine of the crew. The last in line, the first mate, was lost, carried down in the stormy waters as he climbed the mizzenmast to try to escape. The surviving crew sat on the rocky ledge for two days until they were rescued by the tugboat *Edna G.*, which also recovered the mate's body. The wreck now lies in shallow water and is

Tofte Lutsen Grand Marais Grand Portage

often visited by divers. But you might be able to see it too. If the lake is calm and the light is right, they say the outline of the *Madeira* can be seen from above.

The infamous storm of 1905 wrecked the Madeira *and was the final impetus for the construction of Split Rock Lighthouse.*

Gem 25

Crazy Bay at Split Rock Lighthouse State Park

How to Get There: Crazy Bay is located at Split Rock Lighthouse State Park, 20 miles from Two Harbors. To get there, turn right into Split Rock Lighthouse State Park. After purchasing a permit, park at the most distant lot and head toward backpack campsite #3. Turn left down the hill and follow the small dirt trail all the way down to the water through campsite #3.

Accessibility: The unpaved trail is easy, but there's a bit of a climb on the way out. It's not wheelchair accessible.

Cool Things to Know: Want a hidden view of a popular place? Split Rock Lighthouse is one of the most-visited state parks in Minnesota and has been a tourist draw since its completion in 1909, when passengers on the SS *America* fawned over it from the deck and demanded photographs and postcards of the high cliffs. When the first real highway was created in 1923, more crowds gathered and claimed it as their own, forcing the ever-accommodating keepers to give tours on Sundays, in addition to their regular duties. By 1936, the park had already welcomed over 100,000 visitors. You might know all of this already, but despite the many, many visits we have paid to the park, we recently "discovered" a secluded and unique beach with its own tiny harbor. Hidden away near backpack campsite #3, you will discover a lovely sheltered bay with rocks of unusual size and coloration, right on the shores of Crazy Bay (we could uncover no explanation for this moniker). Crazy Bay is just immediately "south" of

Corundum Point, the corundum mining site bought by 3M, which was searching for a natural abrasive. The point provides a great backdrop for sea-gazing, but if the site is occupied, please use good judgment and courtesy when passing by. If it's not, perhaps you'd like to stay for a night at your own private beach?

Crazy Bay at Split Rock Lighthouse State Park is a secluded and unique beach with its own tiny harbor.

Gem 26

Split Rock Lighthouse and State Park

How to Get There: Split Rock Lighthouse is 20 miles from Two Harbors. Follow Highway 61 and turn right to enter the park, which is well marked with brown signs.

Accessibility: The Visitor Center and the Keeper's House are wheelchair accessible, but the fog signal house and lighthouse are not.

Cool Things to Know: Built in 1910 out of a need made apparent during the infamous and devastating Mataafa Storm of 1905, Split Rock Lighthouse State Park now draws hundreds of thousands of visitors from around the world. For a small fee you can take a guided tour right up to the top of the lighthouse and see the light that shines 20-some miles out to sea firsthand. It is now lit only on rare occasions, including every November 10, when it shines out as a beacon and as a memorial to the sailors who lost their lives on the *Edmund Fitzgerald.* To witness the lighting of this breathtakingly beautiful lighthouse is a moving and almost spiritual experience. Split Rock Lighthouse, because of its stark beauty and purposeful stance, is a favorite of calendar makers and has even been seen on *Good Morning, America* as a backdrop to American grandeur. It is Minnesota's own Statue of Liberty; she is our maritime lady with a backbone. To see it is to know it and to love it. Better yet, you can't take a bad picture of the mighty Split Rock Lighthouse, because day or night, sunset or moonrise, it strikes a proud profile. On canvas or in a photograph, the light dances upon the water and the cliff; this lighthouse is beautiful in any weather and in every medium.

To witness the lighting of this breathtakingly beautiful lighthouse perched atop a rocky promontory is a moving and almost spiritual experience.

Gem 27

John Beargrease Indian Cemetery

How to Get There: The John Beargrease Indian Cemetery is 24 miles from Two Harbors. To get there from Highway 61, turn left onto Old Town Road (next to the Holiday gas station in Beaver Bay) and follow the curve to the right. Just before the stop sign, stop and park on the roadside. On your left, there are somewhat concealed steps with a log railing and a faded sign that reads "Indian Burial Ground."

Accessibility: With its steep climb up uneven steps, this site is not wheelchair accessible.

Cool Things to Know: Though he died when her mother was just seven years old, the granddaughter of the famous John Beargrease, Vi Keyport, would be proud to have you visit her grandfather's grave site. She told us that his memory and contribution to the history of the North Shore should be preserved. Immortalized by the internationally renowned sled dog race that bears his name, he kept families and loved ones connected by delivering the U.S. mail throughout the wilderness. During snowy months, his mutt dogs pulled a mail-laden sled; at other times he took to the Lake, and later used a horse and wagon when a rough trail was opened. His father came to Beaver Bay from Cass Lake, but his descendants are proud enrollees of the Grand Portage Band of Lake Superior Chippewa. His living family admits that he had his own personal struggles, but they also point out that he was a vibrant man that was welcomed at any door. The culmination of John Beargrease's service came with his final act of grand

Tofte

Lutsen

Grand Marais

Grand Portage

heroism. He died at Grand Portage in 1910 after rescuing another man in distress on the Lake. He was said to have died soon after due to exposure and a bout of "consumption." There are no individual headstones here, so step lightly. Be sure to read the names listed on the Lake County Historical Marker, and remember this inspiring man who endured many hardships and who brought news to so many.

This Lake County Historical Marker, placed in 1932, marks the names of Indians buried there, including John Beargrease.

THIS TABLET MARKS THE LOCATION OF AN
OLD CHIPPAWA INDIAN CEMETERY
BEGUN ABOUT 1865,
IN WHICH ARE BURIED THE FOLLOWING

ABNOWAH WISHOOP
ANTOINE WISHOOP
JOE MORRISON
THOMAS WISHOOP
EDWARD WISHOOP
JOE YELLOWBIRD
SUSAN WISHOOP
AGNES WISHOOP
PETER GRASSHOPPER
NARCISSE WISHOOP
LIZZIE WISHOOP

CECELIA BLUSKY
NANCY WISHOOP
LIZA WISHOOP
REUBEN BEARGREASE
ANTOINE BEARGREASE
MARY RABBIT
JOE BEARGREASE
JOHN BEARGREASE
THOMAS ESTAIN
NANCY BEARGREASE
MRS. YELLOWBIRD

ERECTED BY
LAKE COUNTY HISTORICAL SOCIETY
AUGUST 20, 1932

50 miles from Duluth

28
EXIT HERE

Silver Bay
Silver Bay Marina,
Safe Harbor

Beaver Bay

Two Harbors

Duluth

Gem 28

Silver Bay Marina, Safe Harbor

How to Get There: Silver Bay Marina and Safe Harbor is 1.7 miles north of Beaver Bay. Immediately after East Beaver Bay, turn right at the signs.

Accessibility: It's easily accessible, but the road to the marina includes a quick turn, which can be dicey at times, so use caution. The road also experiences a high volume of traffic throughout the summer months.

Cool Things to Know: This full-service marina and safe harbor is relatively new to the North Shore. Completed in 1999, it boasts 108 slips, as well as showers, bathrooms, laundry facilities, and concessions. The main marina building includes a sweeping deck with tables and chairs. The grounds also include a scenic overlook at the end of a short trail. Here you can watch the massive ore carriers entering, loading, and departing from Northshore Mining's nearby docks. There are scattered picnic areas, some of which are sheltered, a small beach, and plenty of parking. For scuba divers, the wreck of the *Hesper* lies halfway down the northeastern side of the breakwater in relatively shallow water. The *Hesper* sank in the infamous Mataafa Storm of 1905. The marina is also a popular and productive fishing location; anglers often catch lake trout and salmon not far from the marina. Several sculptures are scattered throughout the marina and add to the experience. All in all, the marina has something for everyone to enjoy, especially day trippers, picnickers, and boaters. The overflow parking lot includes a short trail that leads to a nice overlook of the marina and the working shoreline of the taconite plant. Choose this path for the best

Tofte

Lutsen

Grand Marais

Grand Portage

view of the ore boats being loaded here. Even without a boat of your own, the marina is a great place to boat watch, which is the next best thing to being on one!

All in all, the marina has something for everyone to enjoy, especially day trippers, picnickers, and boaters.

Silver Bay
Rocky Taconite
Beaver Bay
Two Harbors
Duluth

Gem 29

Rocky Taconite

How to Get There: Rocky Taconite is located 3.3 miles north of Beaver Bay. Turn left into the town of Silver Bay on County Road 5 and follow it for one block; the statue is on the right.

Accessibility: The area is accessible for everyone.

Cool Things to Know: Rocky Taconite is a small monument to the taconite industry that, for better or worse, has shaped the cultural landscape around here for the past 100-plus years. Rocky is a chipper, photogenic, jauntily-posed fellow in black and red and a great example of Minnesotan Americana. Dedicated in 1964 as an emissary for the "Taconite Capital of the World," he wields a pick rumored to have come from old Sweden, a nod to the heritage of the many Scandinavians who settled here and whose many descendants still reside here. Rocky Taconite stands at his post as a friendly ambassador to Silver Bay. The city of Silver Bay was built in 1956 as a planned community, a company town to house the workers at the new taconite processing plant. The geographical location was ideal because of its port and the large amount of water it provided. The town is also an example of the conflicts inherent in development on the North Shore. On one hand, the people here needed jobs in order to feed and clothe their families, but these industries sometimes caused damage to the natural world. But the hardworking local people and towns wouldn't be here without that industry. Silver Bay is a reminder that we must make sound decisions, decisions that provide us with the things we need but also protect the environment that enriches our lives.

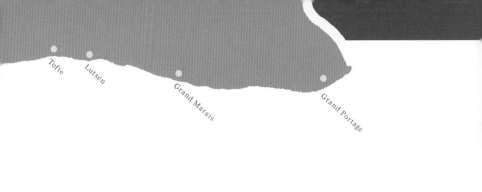

Tofte · Lutsen · Grand Marais · Grand Portage

Rocky Taconite was dedicated in 1964 as an emissary for the "Taconite Capital of the World."

Gem 30

Bean and Bear Lakes

How to Get There: Take the turn into Silver Bay from the stop-light on Highway 61. That will take you on to Outer Drive/County Road 5. Travel 2.3 miles as the road turns into Penn Boulevard/County Road 11, then turn right into a paved parking area marked "Superior Hiking Trail Parking." There are many points of interest on this trail, but the hike to the most dramatic view of Bean Lake is 2.7 miles.

Another option is to stop at the visitor information center run by the Bay Area Historical Center right in town, park in their lot and hike in from there; it's about 3.1 miles to Bean Lake. Both trail options lead you to a trail loop; hiking the whole loop brings your hike up to about 6.5 miles. Follow the blue arrows painted on the rocks on the path.

Accessibility: This trail is rugged and filled with just about every type of terrain short of straight-up rock climbing. Depending on your inclination for speed, or level of physical fitness, plan for about an hour to traverse a mile on this trail.

Cool Things to Know: Difficulty aside, this site is amazing. Also known as the Twin Lakes, Bean and Bear Lakes are sparkling gems set in deep canyons. Seeing them is well worth the effort. However, be advised that while there is only about 400 feet of elevation difference between the trailhead and the highest peak on the trail, there are a great deal of ups and downs throughout the hike, so be prepared for that.

All along the hike, fantastic views of Lake Superior are plentiful, and when you get to the lakes themselves, the almost alpine views from the soaring cliff tops will leave you breathless with awe.

Seldom can you be so close to civilization but in such a remote place. However, don't let the proximity of Duluth (just 30 miles away) fool you; you'll need to bring a map and a GPS, as some of the trail junctions are poorly marked, and other trails (ATV and maintenance roads) cross your path and can be confusing.

The stunning view is well worth the hike.

50 miles from Duluth **31**
EXIT HERE

Silver Bay
Tettegouche Camp
Beaver Bay

Two Harbors

Duluth

Gem 31

Tettegouche Camp

How to Get There: Turn left into Silver Bay at the stoplight on Highway 61, on Outer Drive/County Road 5. Follow that road as it turns into Penn Boulevard/County Road 11 for a total of 5.5 miles, turn right onto Lax Lake Road and go 3.5 miles to the parking area for Tettegouche Camp on your right. From there hike, 1.7 miles into Tettegouche Camp.

For a longer, more gradual 3.5-mile route, travel 4.5 miles past Silver Bay turn right and park at the Tettegouche State Park main trailhead. Note: A state park permit is necessary for both approaches.

Accessibility: The camp is not wheelchair accessible. There's a long steep walk with several benches to rest along the way, but it's on a wide, relatively even gravel surface.

Cool Things to Know: The coolest thing about Tettegouche Camp is crossing the ridge and catching the first glimpse of the hidden lakes found here. You may be familiar with Lake Superior's shoreline, but this is a whole new experience.

Originally the Tettegouche Club, this spot was never logged off and centuries-old white pine abide here on the shore of Micmac Lake, and with Tettegouche and Nipisiquit Lakes a short stroll away. In 1910 a group of sportsman bought the acreage from the logging company and built a lodge, dining hall, and boathouse. Now listed on the National Register of Historic Places, it became a state park in 1979. The four remaining cabins and the historic lodge are reminders of a bygone era and can be rented. A new bathhouse, docks, and canoes are amenities for visitors. Be prepared to pack in/out all your gear, whether fair weather or

Tofte

Lutsen

Grand Marais

Grand Portage

snow, and pump water by hand, but split wood is available for the fire ring. Electricity is available in the cabins as well.

If you make it a day hike, visit in late fall, as the area is home to an uncommon pocket of oaks that draw in fans of fall colors, as well as the moose and bears that forage for acorns.

A private wilderness paradise.

50 miles from Duluth

32
EXIT HERE

Silver Bay
Black Beach
at Silver Bay
Beaver Bay

Two Harbors

Duluth

Gem 32

Black Beach at Silver Bay

How to Get There: To visit Black Beach, travel just a half mile past the turn-off for Silver Bay. Turn right at the brown DNR sign onto Mensing Drive. Go past the business park to a green sign saying "Black Beach" and turn right onto West Lakeview Drive. When the gravel road reaches a T, turn right at another green sign for the beach and travel a half mile until the road ends at the parking lot.

Accessibility: The trail is moderately difficult but short: it's not wheelchair accessible.

Cool Things to Know: Visiting this beach is a strange experience, one that might serve as a reminder to us all to tread lightly on this planet. The only black beach we have seen on the North Shore, it seems exotic, especially in contrast to the reddish hue of a nearby island. The beach's dark coloration is not natural; rather, it came about as a result of the taconite tailings that were dumped in the water offshore. Taconite is low-grade iron ore, which is mined on the Iron Range, 50 to 80 miles from here. The ore is refined, processed, and then baked, creating taconite pellets which are small and easy to transport. The tailings are the remnants of this process; tailings were dumped into the Lake here for about 25 years. This continued until locals, especially commercial fisher-men, protested. One fisherman said that within a few years water clarity had diminished to "just a foot or so" from an original water clarity of about 55 feet. This pushed the herring and other fish miles offshore. Dumping ceased around 1980 and since then the tailings have been disposed of in a land-based disposal basin. The fight to clean up the

Tofte

Lutsen

Grand Marais

Grand Portage

Lake was contentious; many families depended on the plant for their work and survival. But within five years, the water cleared and the fish returned to the area. So when you visit, keep in mind how we can change things for the better, if the cause is right.

The only black beach we have seen on the North Shore, it is exotic and contrasts greatly with the reddish hue of a nearby island.

Gem 33   CLASSIC SITE

Palisade Head

How to Get There: Palisade Head is 3 miles north of Silver Bay. To get there, turn right off of Highway 61 at the green sign that reads "Palisade Head," just before the Palisade Creek bridge. Follow that paved, narrow, steep road as it winds up and back toward the Lake. It will take you to the parking lot where you can walk out onto the cliff itself.

Accessibility: Extreme caution should be exercised here; there are no railings or room for missteps. It is a short walk to the cliff from the lot, on uneven terrain, and you are very high up over the water. The area is not wheelchair accessible.

Cool Things to Know: Palisade Head is at a pullout just outside of the town of Silver Bay. Tettegouche State Park is the entity responsible for managing this scenic outcropping. Marked only with a modest sign, it is an unparalleled place to stand at a great height and take in the awesome view. An extension of the nearby age-old Sawtooth Mountains, Palisade Head is an outcropping of ancient rhyolite and is not to be rivaled by any location on the Great Lakes. It's almost a sin to miss this panoramic view of the North Shore. Once a land of volcanoes and lava, time and temperate weather have made it accessible to human travelers. Standing here is a sublime experience; you realize your frailty and good fortune to be in the right place at the right time, but don't forget that majesty and danger stand side by side—you are required to use all your senses to be safe. Be sure to watch the little ones closely here; there are no fences or railings to remind you where the edges are. But this place is worth the risk; it's an excellent place for a photo shoot, and you will be able to see for miles.

On a clear day you just may be lucky enough to see the edge of the Apostle Islands across the great expanse of water.

On a clear day you just may be lucky enough to see the edge of the Apostle Islands across the great expanse of water.

Duluth

Two Harbors

Beaver Bay

Silver Bay

Trail to
Shovel Point
at Tettegouche
State Park

Gem 34

Trail to Shovel Point at Tettegouche State Park

How to Get There: Turn off of Hwy 61 into the parking area for the combined Tettegouche State Park Visitor Center/Rest Area, 4 miles north of Silver Bay. The trail starts near the Visitor Center. A state park permit isn't required to park in the main lot, but one is needed to drive through the rest of the park.

Accessibility: If you're afraid of heights, this might not be the place for you. In addition, be sure to keep an eye on children and pets here, as sections of the trail are very narrow and there are steep cliffs. The trail is not wheelchair accessible.

Cool Things to Know: The trail to Shovel Point is an hour-long round trip and strenuous at times, but it's worth the effort, as you'll be rewarded with spectacular views and stunning heights. The trail is approximately three-quarters of a mile long and follows the Lake for a quarter mile, culminating at Shovel Point, which looks down on the towering palisades of the shoreline. These palisades are reddish lava formations and the cliffs are made up of porphyritic felsite that has naturally fractured into giant six-sided columns. These vistas are within Tettegouche State Park, which was named by the Micmac Indians brought here to work in logging camps at the turn of the century. The accompanying photo shows the awesome view that you will find at the head of this special trail. Here, and all along the way, you will catch different perspectives of the dramatic outlet of the Baptism River, first called "Au Bapteme" by the French missionaries, because they used its waters in the baptisms of the native peoples. The famous stone arch (see before-and-after photo below) at Shovel Point collapsed in 2010, leaving an impressive stone column. There is much to take in here, and the sense of being high above it all is spine-tingling, but not for the faint-hearted!

In 2010, the famous stone arch that extended above the lake here collapsed, leaving a remarkable stone column.

55 miles from Duluth **35** EXIT HERE

Crystal Beach

Silver Bay

Beaver Bay

Two Harbors

Duluth

Gem 35

Crystal Beach

How to Get There: Just a quarter mile past Highway 1 and 5 miles north of Silver Bay, cross the "overpass" for Crystal Creek (marked by a small green sign) and find the gravelly pullout about 150 yards beyond on the right. Scout around a bit and find the narrow and winding trail.

Accessibility: There is a steep hike to the beach. The path is difficult, covered with shale, and not wheelchair accessible.

Cool Things to Know: Flowing out from the surrounding hills, Crystal Creek is full of beautiful, multicolored stones and the beach itself is truly majestic. Gnarled northern white cedar trees cling to the nearby cliff faces, and the sea caves tucked beneath them seem to shelter secrets or hidden treasure. This is perhaps why the founders of 3M, a company that would later become one of the most powerful corporations on the planet, chose this location to mine for minerals. Here they discovered what they believed was corundum—an ideal abrasive stone—one they could use to mass-produce grinding wheels and to fashion their own variant of sandpaper. 3M even went so far as to build a foundry and dock alongside Crystal Creek. They spent a year mining what they thought was corundum. Finally in the winter of 1903–04 they shipped a ton of the ore to Duluth, only to discover their geologists had made a mistake and the ore was useless. The site was quickly dismantled and abandoned. Such are the unlikely beginnings of a corporate empire. Today the moss-covered remains of the old foundation are still here; they are an interesting diversion as you make your way down to the beach. It's worth the trek, as

Tofte

Lutsen

Grand Marais

Grand Portage

something about the place makes one dream big. If you're like us, you'll find it difficult to leave this storied place.

Flowing out from the surrounding hills, Crystal Creek is full of beautiful, multicolored stones, and the beach itself is truly majestic.

Gem 36

Illgen Falls

How to Get There: Turn left onto Highway 1, which is about 6.5 miles north of Silver Bay. About 1.5 miles up the road, park at the pullout on the left, just after the guardrail. The Illgen Falls Trail starts at the pullout.

Accessibility: The trail is uneven, unpaved, but short. It's not wheelchair accessible.

Cool Things to Know: If you've never heard of Illgen City, it's only because you live in the wrong century. At one time, this inauspicious location sported the finest hotel to be found between Duluth and Thunder Bay. The Aztec, in its heyday, looked like something that belonged in Atlantic City, or maybe Chicago. A man by the name of Illgen, its builder, was something of a world traveler and fancied that his hotel had a flavor reflecting the inns of Old Mexico. Built in 1924, it included a large bar, complete with slot machines and expensive liquors. Local legend says Chicago's criminal elite and even Al Capone stopped by on their way to secret northern lodges where they evaded G-men and caught up on their fishing. From the trailhead, take the steep but short walk behind the cabin, which is available for rent through Tettegouche State Park (see page 80) and find an Eden-like scene before you. Your efforts will reveal the top of a tall waterfall, impressive even during the drought when we photographed it. The waters of Baptism River fall into a huge, dark pool underneath—a beautiful and glorious sight. Surrounded by huge, round boulders, the falls plummet 30 feet and have been immortalized by a German immigrant whose painting of the falls is preserved on the walls of an antique store in old downtown Two Harbors. Explore the top of the falls if you will; if you want to get a snapshot of the view we show here, you'll need to do some scrambling on a pretty rough trail.

The waters of the Baptism River fall into a huge, dark pool underneath—a beautiful and glorious sight.

Gem 37

Wolf Ridge Environmental Learning Center

How to Get There: At the junction of Highway 61 and County Road 6 (also called Little Marais Road), turn onto County Road 6, heading away from the lake. Proceed 4 miles down County Road 6, and turn left on Cranberry Road. The turn is well marked with signs for Wolf Ridge. Follow the small gravel driveway for about 2 miles, passing Wolf Ridge Farm and Wolf Ridge Forest Ecology site, to reach the main campus. Just before you reach the main campus buildings you'll see Wolf Lake, a sparkling gem that will make you catch your breath.

Accessibility: Some areas are wheelchair accessible. The trails nearest the campus are easy, with moderate loop trails meandering further.

Cool Things to Know: A global leader in sustainability, Wolf Ridge has been dedicated to environmental education since 1971. Situated on 2,000 acres between the Boundary Waters Canoe Area Wilderness and Lake Superior, this site is all about learning and connecting with the natural world.

Always popular with students and researchers, Wolf Ridge encourages the public to visit in any season during office hours: Monday through Friday, 8 a.m. to 4 p.m. Park in one of the lots and pick up a trail for hiking, cross-country skiing, or snowshoeing; there are 18 miles in all.

You can also visit the Science Center displays, nearby scenic overlooks, or see if programs involving the resident raptors

Tofte

Lutsen

Grand Marais

Grand Portage

Wolf Ridge Environmental Learning Center

and other teaching animals are on the schedule. There's
even an aquarium. Drop-in visitors are invited to the annual
open house and bird-banding activities in the early summer.
Check their website for dates at https://wolf-ridge.org/.

A look at stunning Wolf Lake.

Gem 38

Sugarloaf Cove

How to Get There: Located 19 miles north of Silver Bay, and 5 miles south of Schroeder, look for a brown "Sugarloaf Cove" sign and carefully turn off Highway 61 and toward the Lake at milepost 73. The log interpretive center is just down the hill from the parking lot.

Accessibility: It's possible to drive directly to the interpretive center, and wheelchair ramps are available. However, while steps and railings provide support to the beach trail, it is not paved. Other trails on the property are relatively wide and flat, with benches and some steps added for increased accessibility. Trails are open during daylight hours; the building hours vary by season.

Cool Things to Know: This is a place where ancient history and the recent past meet. The cobblestone beach features 1.1 billion-year-old lava flows, including pahoehoe, a Hawaiian term referring to lava that occurs in whirled, swirly formations.

The cove is also a great place to learn more about the area's long logging history. The site was owned by Consolidated Paper from the 1940s through the 1970s and prized for its sheltered cove. The cove was used as a log landing site, and huge rafts of logs were bundled and towed by steam-driven tugboats across Lake Superior to Ashland for processing. You can still see traces of the logging operations on site, including metal mooring rings, a root cellar, and boom logs.

Sugarloaf Cove has been managed by the North Shore Stewardship Association since 1992, and the organization

Tofte

Lutsen

Sugarloaf Cave

Grand Marais

Grand Portage

is dedicated to restoring and preserving the North Shore's forests and ecosystems. The site's interpretive center offers naturalist education programs on a number of topics, including winter camping, birding workshops, and plant identification classes, throughout the year.

A picture-perfect Lake Superior scene.

Gem 39

Taconite Harbor

How to Get There: Taconite Harbor is 22 miles north of Silver Bay, just before mile marker 77. To visit, turn right at the entrance, which is marked with a sign.

Accessibility: There is a paved parking lot in the exhibit area; other areas are not wheelchair accessible.

Cool Things to Know: As you leave Highway 61 and pass along the long drive down to the harbor, you will drive through a ghost town first. The wide, weed-covered open spaces give you an eerie sense of something missing. Indeed, there were once homes here and a taconite plant, all part of a complete little town. The 24 prefabricated homes are gone now, but you can still see sections of the old streets, and a couple of defunct streetlights hang above now-empty spaces. Farther down the road, you will pass a display of sorts, the likes of which you will seldom find elsewhere; it consists of heavy equipment used in the iron ore and shipping industries. There are four huge items with signage that explains their functions and history, including a massive scoop and an 8-foot-high tire from an 85-ton dump truck. Two massive anchors are also here; one, from the ore-carrier *Bethlehem*, weighs in at 7,000 pounds. The other, from the *Butterfield*, includes the anchor and capstan. The *Butterfield* was a tug and used as a "lumber hooker" from 1919 to 1957 and spent two years in military service. All these artifacts are a preface of what you came to see—the harbor itself. In order to create a harbor, two natural islands were used as anchors and a breakwall was built between them. Early maps labeled this place as "Two Island River." Once used for shipping

39
EXIT HERE

73 miles from Duluth

Tofte
Lutsen
Taconite Harbor
Grand Marais
Grand Portage

taconite, the old site has now been converted to a power plant. The harbor is now used as a public water access site and a safe harbor.

In order to create a harbor, two natural islands were used as anchors and a breakwall was built between them.

Gem 40

Father Baraga's Cross

How to Get There: Father Baraga's Cross is in the town of Schroeder, 26 miles north of Silver Bay. After crossing the Cross River Bridge, look for a small sign on the right hand side of the road. Follow the road to the small parking area.

Accessibility: Follow the narrow dirt path a short distance from the parking area. There is a short, but winding, path consisting of crushed rock.

Cool Things to Know: In 1846, Father Baraga, a missionary priest, undertook his voyage from the far shores of the Apostle Islands on a mission of mercy. News had reached him that the Anishinabe people at Grand Portage were sick. He and his lone companion, Dubois, left Madeline Island in a small wooden vessel equipped with oars and a single sail. The trip of 40 miles was nearly undone when a strong storm came up as they were halfway across the Lake. Father Baraga prayed fervently for safe passage and the storm broke. The two arrived safely at the mouth of what is now called the Cross River. The river was named after the modest wooden cross Father Baraga and his companion erected in gratitude on an outcropping overlooking the Lake and the river mouth. Today a granite replacement forever commemorates his brave and honorable voyage. During the summer months, church services are held at the foot of the cross, and congregants sit on the rock shelf below. It is hard to imagine a more beautiful church than the shore of Lake Superior, which has received the prayers of multitudes from every faith.

40 EXIT HERE   76 miles from Duluth

Tofte

Lutsen

Grand Marais

Grand Portage

Father Baraga's Cross

Father Baraga erected a modest wooden cross here at the mouth of the Cross River in gratitude for safe passage.

Gem 41

Cross River Heritage Center

How to Get There: The Heritage Center is in the town of
Schroeder at milepost 79. Located 26 miles north of
Silver Bay, it's about halfway between Duluth and Canada.

Accessibility: The area has no accessibility problems.

Cool Things to Know: A landmark building, completed in
1929, the Cross River Heritage Center is the only example
of Tudor-style architecture in Cook County. The original
wood floor and stone fireplace are intact. The building has
been an inn, a general store, and a boarding house, among
other things. Recently renovated and run by the Schroeder
Area Historical Society, the Heritage Center is dedicated to
preserving and sharing the cultural history of the area.
Their gift shop is exceptional and carries artwork by
regional artisans. Their exhibits of photographs, memora-
bilia, and artifacts of early pioneer days are fun to look
through, and it's always interesting to place yourself in the
shoes of a pioneer and try to imagine what you would have
had to endure "back then." One of the Center's primary goals
is to educate visitors about the work of renowned architect
Edwin Lundie. From the 1940s through the 1960s, Lundie
designed and built 17 cabins and summer homes along
an 80-mile stretch of the North Shore. The Cross River
Heritage Center documents his work and offers annual
tours of a selection of these buildings, all of which benefited
from Lundie's devotion to detail and love of fine craftsman-
ship. Lundie drew heavily from Scandinavian influences—
incorporating carved pillars and heavy, visible timbers.
The Cross River Heritage Center offers you and your family

41 76 miles from Duluth
EXIT HERE

Cross River
Heritage Center

Tofte

Lutsen

Grand Marais

Grand Portage

a chance to step inside the past. Two rooms that have been restored to period styles can be toured and leave you free to imagine spending a night at the old Inn in a time when the wilderness was just opening up to tourism.

A landmark building completed in 1929, the Cross River Heritage Center is the only Tudor-style architecture in Cook County.

Gem 42

Temperance River, Cauldron Trail

How to Get There: Located 1 mile north of Schroeder. Go over the Temperance River Bridge. Just before the state park entrance, park on either side. This trail is not on the lakeside.

Accessibility: The first quarter mile of the trail is paved and wheelchair accessible. Beyond that point it becomes a moderately difficult climb up the rocks of the gorge. Please take children in hand, as there is no guardrail along this powerful river.

Cool Things to Know: The water of the Temperance River swirls mightily, carving potholes in the ancient rock. Originating from its source in the Boundary Waters Canoe Area Wilderness, Brule Lake feeds this waterway. In its last half mile, the river descends a grand total of 160 feet. To clear up the name of this river—when the river was named it was said to be the only river on the North Shore without a sand "bar" at its mouth. Perhaps it is different than most; however, a sand bar does form here at times, and other rivers of the shore have them sometimes, but not always. Whether you only stroll the first quarter mile or venture farther up the rocks to the most common turnaround point (about a 1.5-mile round trip), you'll witness a miniature canyon gouged out of solid rock. It features a great cauldron that was cut away over thousands and thousands of years by the relentless water. The canyon is even grander at its base or from above, if you choose to make the short climb. Every bend of the river offers

42 EXIT HERE 77 miles from Duluth

Tofte

Lutsen

Temperance River,
Cauldron Trail,

Grand Marais

Grand Portage

unique sights—sights the old cedars and pines have been witness to for many years.

If you have time, don't miss the waterfall below the Highway 61 bridge, accessible from the pullout on the other side of the highway.

On the Cauldron Trail, you'll witness a miniature canyon gouged out of solid rock.

Gem 43

North Shore Commercial Fishing Museum

How to Get There: Located in the town of Tofte, at the junction of the Sawbill Trail and Highway 61. For details, visit www.commercialfishingmuseum.org.

Accessibility: The museum has no accessibility problems.

Cool Things to Know: Commercial fishing was at its peak from the 1880s through the 1950s on Lake Superior. This great little museum helps bring that history to life and houses many interesting tools and artifacts. The collection includes a beautifully restored full-scale boat from the heyday of commercial fishing, and the many enlarged black and white photos on display here offer a stark look at how difficult life—and even survival—could be in this sometimes unforgiving and isolating wilderness. The museum helps preserve that important story by collecting the stories of the pioneer families that worked and lived here. By documenting the daily lives of these folks, the museum gives us a view into days gone by and a sense of the struggle and tenacity of these hardworking people. The fishermen that arrived on the North Shore were often of Norwegian and Swedish descent—countries with a long history of fishing. These men (and women) were fine craftsmen and demonstrated a good deal of ingenuity, as seen in the many tools of the trade found in this worthwhile historical archive.

43 EXIT HERE

78 miles from Duluth

Tofte
North Shore Commercial
Fishing Museum

Lutsen

Grand Marais

Grand Portage

The North Shore Commercial Fishing Museum offers a stark look at the reality of survival in this sometimes unforgiving and isolating wilderness.

Gem 44

Butterwort Cliffs Scientific & Natural Area

How to Get There: At milepost 101 on Highway 61, turn left into the main entrance at Cascade River State Park. There you can purchase a day-use permit; if you miss the office hours you can purchase a permit from a self-service pay station. Once your permit is in hand, travel south on Highway 61 to the Cascade River State Park Picnic Area, which is just past milepost 100. There is ample parking available there.

Accessibility: The dirt walking path from the picnic area parking to the beach is wide and easy to navigate. The beach is strewn with large boulders.

Cool Things to Know: Designated a Scientific and Natural Area (SNA), Butterwort Cliffs lies within Cascade River State Park and preserves a narrow strip of rocky shore that is home to an uncommon natural community. The moist, cool climate is home to a variety of rare wildlife, from brightly colored lichens to an unusual variety of butterwort.

The butterwort, for which the area is named, is a carnivorous plant. It grows in fragile mats, and its sticky leaves trap insects, enabling butterwort to absorb their nutrients. Butterwort is very rare; in Minnesota, it only grows on these few acres of sheltered, rocky shoreline.

The unique subarctic microhabitat of Butterwort Cliffs is fragile, and access to the Cliffs themselves is restricted from May 1st to August 15th to protect nesting bird colonies. However, the picnic area and beach, which we're leading you to here, remain open year-round.

44
EXIT HERE

95 miles from Duluth

Tofte

Lutsen

Butterwort Cliffs
Scientific & Natural Area

Grand Marais

Grand Portage

Well worth a visit for all its own attractions, the picnic area here is a special one, with sloping paths down to a generous bit of forest before the beach. Several picnic tables and fire rings are scattered below the boughs of some of the grandest northern white cedar trees on the north shore, giving an ancient feel to the subdued and serene area.

The rocky beach at Butterwort Cliffs.

Gem 45

Cutface Creek Pullout at Good Harbor Bay

How to Get There: The Cutface Creek Pullout is 14 miles north of Lutsen. Turn right into the parking lot at mile marker 104.

Accessibility: The area is wide open except for the short dip down to the beach. Pathways are paved and extend to the picnic area, but the beach isn't wheelchair accessible.

Cool Things to Know: Above Good Harbor Bay is the small Cutface Creek wayside rest, where the construction of the highway cut away into one of the few sandstone beds (overlaid with lava) on this side of the Lake. If you are lucky, you might find thomsonite washed up on the north side of the bay. Named in 1820 for chemist Thomas Thomson of Scotland, this rock is a rare and prized gemstone the world over. Folklore states that Queen Victoria was so fond of it that when it became harder to find on the shores of Scotland, she supposedly commissioned Native people of the North Shore to collect it for her. Most finds are tiny pebbles. You might recognize it by its unique green and pink swirling bands that were formed in pockets of basalt during a single lava event. This 6-mile stretch is one of the only beaches where you will find this gem on the North Shore. In addition to the lure of a treasure hunt, this site also has other, more practical draws. The site is a well-laid-out wayside rest and includes benches, paved walkways, picnic tables, permanent restroom facilities, and a pet exercise area. Those things are nice, but it's the allure of unearthing riches that makes us go back! Spend a few minutes or a few hours exploring Cutface

Creek and the beaches of Good Harbor Bay. Even if you don't come away with riches, you will nonetheless be richer for the time spent here.

This 6-mile stretch is one of the only beaches on the North Shore where you will find the treasured thomsonite stone.

Gem 46

Lightkeeper's House— Cook County Historical Society Museum

How to Get There: In Grand Marais (18 miles north of Lutsen) turn right onto Broadway Avenue and proceed about two blocks to just past the intersection of Wisconsin Street. The museum will be on your left.

Accessibility: The museum is not wheelchair accessible. There is a short flight of steps at the entry and a long staircase to exhibits on the second floor.

Cool Things to Know: Here you will discover thrilling true tales of wilderness survival and sea adventures. Better yet, visiting is free!

Grand Marais was the site of some of the first European settlements in Minnesota; nonetheless it is still solidly on the edge of the wilderness, even today. Listed on the National Register of Historic Places, the Lightkeeper's house in Grand Marais was built in 1896. Now a museum for the Cook County Historical Society, displays throughout the building usher visitors through visual and audio experiences detailing the area's history of logging, commercial fishing, and the importance of the Anishinaabe people to the region.

In addition to the 1885 Fresnel lens that lit the first lighthouse, many artifacts, archives, and photographs are on display. With a long history of a thriving artists' colony in Grand Marais, many excellent paintings are also shown here.

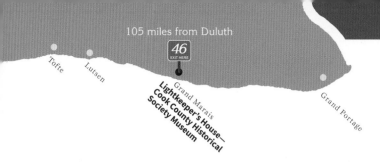

46
EXIT HERE

Tofte

Lutsen

Grand Marais
Lightkeeper's House—
Cook County Historical
Society Museum

Grand Portage

From May to October, the museum is open Tuesdays through Saturdays from 10 a.m. to 4 p.m. During the rest of the year it is open Fridays and Saturdays, 10 a.m. to 4 p.m. On Saturdays during the summer, free guided walking tours head out from the museum to Lighthouse Point. Call (218) 387-2883 to double-check the hours or visit www.cookcountyhistory.org.

The lightkeeper's house, now a museum.

Gem 47

Grand Marais Breakwall

How to Get There: Grand Marais is 18 miles north of Lutsen. To get to the breakwall, turn right on Broadway Avenue. At the end of the road you'll be in the Coast Guard parking lot.

Accessibility: The path is a bit bumpy, narrow in places, and downright precarious if you walk the breakwall itself. It's not wheelchair accessible.

Cool Things to Know: The Coast Guard station stands on what was once an island, with only some shallow marshy land between it and solid shore. A manmade peninsula now divides the bay and gives you a chance to walk out to a trail that winds through a small, but complete, boreal forest and ancient lava formations. As you stand on those mammoth rocks it's hard not to gaze out at the harbor and imagine what life was like on the Lake prior to the development of modern safeguards and technology. In fact, a shipwreck in 1881 spurred development of the Grand Marais Safe Harbor and Lighthouse. The schooner *Stranger* wrecked just outside of the harbor and beyond the reach of help; all four crew members perished within sight of warmth and safety. Finally, in 1882, the first breakwater and lighthouse were constructed. Once you walk out onto the breakwall with the Sawtooth Mountains rising gloriously behind the city, you may be inspired to do what you can to help protect such a fine sight.

105 miles from Duluth

47
EXIT HERE

Tofte

Lutsen

Grand Marais
Grand Marais Breakwall

Grand Portage

*Before the construction of the breakwall and lighthouse, the schooner
Stranger wrecked just outside of the harbor in 1881.*

Gem 48

Chippewa City

How to Get There: Chippewa City is one-half mile north of Grand Marais. Look for the brown historical marker. Just outside of town, you'll see an old white church on your right. Pull into its parking lot.

Accessibility: The area is mostly unpaved but it's easy walking. There are no major obstacles to wheelchair access here.

Cool Things to Know: Unfortunately, we have virtually no documentation from the original native residents about this little city. All that remains to tell us what life was like for them are letters and photographs taken by the European settlers that observed them there. From around 1855 until the early 1900s, a number of Anishinabe families lived here, numbering from around 100 people to as many as 200 by the 1915 census. They were the first inhabitants of this land, but they were forced to adapt to a new way of life by the Treaty of 1854 at LaPointe. Hopefully you will visit the site when the lilacs are blooming, like we did; it makes a pretty picture. Built in 1895, the St. Francis Xavier Church is on the National Register of Historic Places and is all that remains standing of Chippewa City. Still, you can probably envision the place surrounded by rough houses and a scattering of traditional aboriginal shelters at the edges. Much of the village was destroyed in 1908 by forest fires. The church was saved by the gunship *Gopher*, which was sent by the federal government to fight the fires, but sadly many of the native children died of smoke inhalation. The native people of this little town were known to create beautiful birch bark baskets that they crafted with

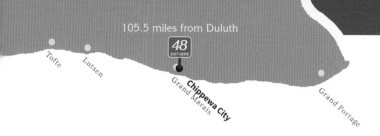

105.5 miles from Duluth

48
EXIT HERE

Tofte

Lutsen

Grand Marais

Chippewa City

Grand Portage

porcupine quills. They also created beaded bags and other art for the townspeople of Grand Marais and other visitors. This church provides us with living proof of their tenacity and ability to survive.

Built in 1895, the St. Francis Xavier Church is on the National Register of Historic Places.

Gem 49

Devil Track River Stonehouse

How to Get There: The Devil Track River Stonehouse is located on the north side of the Devil Track River, just after the bridge that crosses the river. It is about 3 miles north of Grand Marais. When visiting, be careful and don't stop on the bridge. Instead, find a safe place to pull over!

Accessibility: Just look from your car.

Cool Things to Know: Now a private residence, this ultra-cool building is a great photo opportunity. Constructed of large stones taken directly from Lake Superior's shore just below, this structure is unique and reminiscent of an old European mill house. Its outer wall lines up with the river's edge, and it seems to stand guard over the mouth of the river with all the sturdy determination of a fortress. Doris Croft lived there as a child, and her family ran the "Devil's Track Cottages," a resort enterprise. Her husband, Sweenie Croft, remembers when the original building was going up. Only 9 years old in 1932, he can still recall local men doing the backbreaking work of hauling the stones up from the coast. The stonehouse was built on an old bridge abutment. This provided a wonderful view and some degree of stability. Doris's father added the upper story and doubled the lower level, and she can recall her younger brother complaining about having to carry cobblestones from the beach for the addition. Doris remembers the lake home as a warm, lovely place, with an unbeatable view of the water.

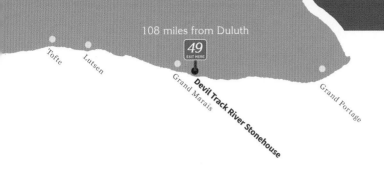

108 miles from Duluth

49 EXIT HERE

Tofte

Lutsen

Grand Marais

Devil Track River Stonehouse

Grand Portage

Constructed in 1932 of large stones taken directly from Lake Superior's shore just below, this building was the lodge for cottage renters.

Gem 50

Paradise Beach at Colvill

How to Get There: The pullout is just north of the Kadunce River, 8.5 miles north of Grand Marais. It starts just south of Colvill and extends for 5 miles to milepost 123.

Accessibility: It is a short walk to the beach, but the beach isn't wheelchair accessible.

Cool Things to Know: The elusive "Paradise Beach Agate" is known by rock-hunting junkies as a highly desirable stone to own. This long and lonely beach is a great place to stroll leisurely and relax or burn off all those extra calories you've accumulated while sampling the local fare. Paradise Beach goes on and on, but if you want more, it's close to an entry point to the Superior Hiking Trail. In addition, the beach boasts a historic marker, paved parking, and picnic tables for that lakeside meal. Food never tastes better than at the shore in the open air. The lack of superfluous amenities is part of the charm; this keeps the crowds away, and after all, that's what we are looking for in a beach. While private development cuts away at the shores, we must cherish such quiet places and do whatever we can to keep them peaceful and free. Here at Paradise Beach you will have miles to ponder important matters or let your mind wander lazily if that's what you need. The ongoing expanse of this beach should give you lots of time to reflect, wander, or just enjoy the moment.

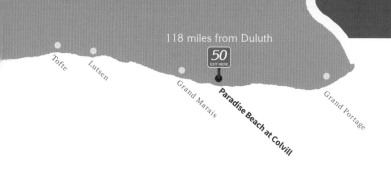

118 miles from Duluth

50
EXIT HERE

Tofte

Lutsen

Grand Marais

Paradise Beach at Colvill

Grand Portage

This long and lonely beach is a great place to stroll in a leisurely fashion.

Gem 51

Kadunce Creek and Trail

How to Get There: About 8.5 miles north of Grand Marais, just past milepost 118, there is a parking area on the lake side of Highway 61. Often referred to as Kadunce Creek, this waterway is officially named Kadunce River and you will park in the Kadunce River State Wayside. From the parking area, cross Highway 61 to reach the trailhead.

Accessibility: The trails along the creek are fairly easy for most of the way, but if you want to scramble down into the gorge, it's a steep climb.

Cool Things to Know: Designated a high-quality habitat for steelhead and brook trout, Kadunce Creek has long been a favorite of anglers. However, the 1.2-mile out-and-back trail runs along the stream and is easygoing enough for just about anyone to enjoy. (It's also a spur of the Superior Hiking Trail.)

One of five state waysides managed by the Minnesota Department of Natural Resources on the north shore, the Kadunce River State Wayside is too small to be a state park, but it has unique cultural and natural resources that put it in a class of its own.

If you keep strictly to the trail, you will find much to appreciate, like several waterfalls and secretive caves. Venturing into the stream itself is an option, but keep in mind that the Kadunce, like all waterways, has the potential to be filled with rushing water. So don't wade during the spring melt or after heavy rains.

118 miles from Duluth

51
EXIT HERE

Tofte

Lutsen

Grand Marais

Kadunce Creek
and Trail

Grand Portage

If you wade into the stream amid the deep gorge and mossy rock walls, you'll see a small but remarkable rhyolite canyon upstream, with walls that soar above narrow passageways, often creating dramatic waterfalls. Paradise Beach, located at the mouth of the Kadunce, is also a treat (see page 112.)

The beautiful Kadunce Creek.

Gem 52

Devil's Kettle,
Judge C.R. Magney State Park

How to Get There: Judge C.R. Magney State Park is 14 miles from Grand Marais. On Highway 61, turn left away from the Lake at the signs for the state park.

Accessibility: There is an uphill hike of approximately 1 mile, which is unpaved, requires climbing, and includes many stairs.

Cool Things to Know: The Devil's Kettle might have been called "Mystery Falls." It is said that at the base of the 50-foot falls the water spills into a bottomless opening in the earth. If you ask a park official or local resident where the opening ends up, you will be told, "No one knows." People have tried to find out by sending semi-buoyant floats marked with paint or fabric to see if they could be located again farther downstream or out in the Lake. Thus far, none of these items have ever been rediscovered. Perhaps a series of huge underground caves and tunnels carries the water away to parts unknown. The ancient rock in this area is over 1 billion years old and keeps its secrets. The trip and trail leading to the small wooden platform overlooking Devil's Kettle is breathtakingly beautiful, especially in fall. Red and yellow leaves mix with the constant evergreens and line the path; breaks in the treeline offer spectacular vistas of the Brule River and the surrounding country. Near the trail's end you are met with something of a curiosity—hundreds of wooden stairs that rise and fall, hugging the hills and small canyons, leading toward the trailhead. Frequent rests may

119 miles from Duluth

52
EXIT HERE

Tofte

Lutsen

Grand Marais

Devil's Kettle,
Judge C.R. Magney
State Park

Grand Portage

be necessary for those not equipped with the lungs of a marathoner. But in spite of this, the hike is tough to beat; a sense of the deep forest and wild nature is everywhere. Don't miss this one.

The trail leading to the small wooden platform overlooking Devil's Kettle is breathtakingly beautiful.

Gem 53

Naniboujou Lodge

How to Get There: Turn right just after Judge C.R. Magney State Park. Naniboujou Lodge is located 14 miles north of Grand Marais.

Accessibility: The lodge is wheelchair accessible.

Cool Things to Know: Maintaining a feel for its 1929 beginnings as an exclusive sportsman's club, the Naniboujou is now revitalized, after failing shortly after the stock market's "Black Friday" in 1929. Famous names were associated with the lodge, with Jack Dempsey, Babe Ruth, and Ring Lardner signing up to be part of the developing vacation spot. Preserved as a working business that offers tranquility and restoration, the 24 rooms are without phones or TVs, and visitors are invited to walk the property, sit by the shore, and soak in the solitude of this place.

Listed on the National Register of Historic Places, the lodge houses the largest fireplace made of native rock in Minnesota—it took 200 tons of rock to build! If an overnight stay is not in your plans, drop in for a meal in the stunning Great Hall, where the 20-foot-high domed ceiling and walls are covered in brilliant patterns of vibrant colors. The scene is truly awe-inspiring. During the summer months, the lodge offers afternoon tea (sandwiches, cookies, and scones) for a unique experience, and welcomes anyone who wants to visit.

119 miles from Duluth

53
EXIT HERE

Tofte

Lutsen

Grand Marais

Naniboujou Lodge

Grand Portage

Experience first-class dining in the Great Hall, a one-of-a-kind setting.

Gem 54

Hovland Dock at Chicago Bay

How to Get There: Hovland Dock is 18 miles north of Grand Marais. Follow Highway 61, then turn right onto Chicago Bay Road. Travel less than a quarter mile to the lakeshore and you'll see the dock on your right.

Accessibility: Pull up to it and take pictures; it's an easy stroll to the dock end. Exercise caution if you venture out farther, as parts of the concrete dock are falling away. The dock is not wheelchair accessible.

Cool Things to Know: For such a little and apparently unobtrusive site, this location is rich with history and neat things to see. The old village of Hovland lingers on, and though diminished, it is somehow evident that the heartbeat of the community was a strong one. The dock itself, massive and built for deepwater off-loading, was built in 1905 as the hub of transportation for the packet and passenger ships that came once a week with goods, mail, and passengers. Even back then, Hovland was an early tourist draw, thriving with stores, a school, and lodging accommodations, though the only things left operating now are a post office and a few homes. With commercial fishing and logging as the mainstays of economic stability, the town was once thriving, as lake trout and herring were taken by the boatload. At the end of the dock you can still see evidence of the tracks put in to move heavy crates of fish to a warehouse on shore. The bell that you see at the foot of the dock was rung to signal a ship's arrival and must have stirred up folks on shore with excitement. There are old cottages near the dock that once housed working families.

123 miles from Duluth

54
EXIT HERE

Tofte

Lutsen

Grand Marais

Hovland Dock at Chicago Bay

Grand Portage

See also the historical marker commemorating the "Old Dog Trail," the trek of John Beargrease and others that stopped at Hovland.

The massive dock was built in 1905 for deepwater packet and passenger ships that came once a week.

Gem 55

Two-Fish-House Beach

How to Get There: Two-Fish-House Beach is 34 miles north of Grand Marais. To get there, turn right between mile markers 139 and 140.

Accessibility: This is a moderate walk that's not wheelchair accessible.

Cool Things to Know: This is a beach that features a sweeping grandeur; here it is secluded and stately, and a true gem in that it is undiscovered and almost entirely unknown. The deteriorating fish houses are a few of the memorials to the men and families that worked here to survive, their hardscrabble lives now elevated to romantic status. In their desire for independence and self-sufficiency they often found a way to carve out a niche, surviving because of their resourcefulness and inherent toughness. However, it was a hard life with pennies to the pound for their dangerous and definitely unromantic work on shore—cleaning and hauling their catch. Stroll this beach at a leisurely pace; search for the rare lichens that live here, and reflect on how we are all called to do our piece to keep these rare places pristine for those who will come after us. And as you stand here and look far across the wide, wild water, remember that Lake Superior is connected to the Atlantic Ocean by the St. Lawrence Seaway, and try to put yourself in the settlers' shoes, half a world away from Europe and the homelands they left behind.

55
EXIT HERE

Tofte

Lutsen

Grand Marais

Grand Portage

Two-Fish-House Beach

This is a beach that features a sweeping grandeur. This place is both secluded and stately.

Gem 56

Hollow Rock Resort

How to Get There: Hollow Rock Resort is 6.3 miles north of Reservation River and 36 miles from Grand Marais; turn right at the sign that reads, "Hollow Rock Resort."

Accessibility: The are is easily enjoyed by all. One of the cabins is wheelchair accessible.

Cool Things to Know: This small cabin resort is owned and operated by the Grand Portage Band of Lake Superior Chippewa and is open year-round. There are seven cabins, some of them large enough to accommodate a large group. This 12-acre resort encompasses a small, but beautiful, stretch of the shoreline. We spent a night here in the cabin farthest out on the point; it was close to safety but separate from the world of human chaos. Then in the daylight we explored what felt like our own private tiny peninsula, discovering the thrones and tables the Lake leaves after thousands of years of scouring at every beach. This leaves each beach with its own character, and exploring them renews the sense of discovery one has in the presence of the great Inland Sea. All of this happened before we explored the Hollow Rock itself, which is close enough to shore for you to reach it without getting your feet too wet. We climbed to its peak and stood beneath its arch; it's big enough for a small canoe or kayak to navigate. No matter what temper you may find her in, the myriad moods of the Lake are always beautifully framed by the Hollow Rock.

141 miles from Duluth

56
EXIT HERE

Tofte

Lutsen

Grand Marais

Grand Portage

Hollow Rock Resort

*The myriad moods of the Lake, no matter what temper you may find her
in, are always beautifully framed by the Hollow Rock.*

Gem 57

Grand Portage Marina and Campground

How to Get There: In the town of Grand Portage, turn right off of Highway 61. Signs will direct you to the casino and hotel. This is the same road that brings you to the marina and campground. You will need to make a left turn after passing the new gas station/trading post. This will bring you into the marina and campground area; the main office is located on the west side of the marina.

Accessibility: Easily accessible to all motorized traffic, it lies in a large, flat area and has easy walking surfaces.

Cool Things to Know: While visiting or staying at the Grand Portage Marina and Campground, you will be treated to a nice view of the Lake, and on clear days you can easily see the silhouette of Isle Royale, 12 miles distant. The marina, though small, has character. Surrounded by a wooden boardwalk, small fishing boats used by Native American fisherman are readily visible. The entire Grand Portage area possesses a timeless, old-world feel. Whether staying in an RV or a tent, as we did, you can know that voyageurs and the Native Anishinabe people have used the same ground to bivouac and camp for years. Any artifacts chanced upon should be given to a tribal representative or brought to the staff at Grand Portage National Monument located nearby. During our stay we were awakened in the early morning hours by the whistles and soft grunts of a family of otters, no doubt drawn by the ample smells of fresh fish. They entered the marina mouth like a small flotilla of boats, investigated a

Tofte

Lutsen

Grand Marais

144 miles from Duluth **57** EXIT HERE

Grand Portage Marina and Campground

Grand Portage

few locations on the boardwalk, found little, and left as they had arrived: chirping and whistling, off to other adventures.

The entire Grand Portage area possesses a timeless and an old-world feel.

Gem 58

Grand Portage National Monument Heritage Center

How to Get There: Turn right just before the Grand Portage gas station, then left at the four-way stop onto Mile Creek Road. Travel just a quarter mile farther. The monument will be on your left; it is 39 miles north of Grand Marais.

Accessibility: The center is wheelchair accessible.

Cool Things to Know: The National Park Service and the Grand Portage Band of Ojibwe have joined efforts to maintain and operate Grand Portage National Monument. The new, multi-million dollar Heritage Center opened in 2007 to help visitors understand and interpret this valuable site. Together, the two entities run a summer mentoring program for Grand Portage youth, maintain the cultural and historical accuracy of the information shared with visitors, and preserve Native artifacts and art. Renowned painter Carl Gawboy, of the Bois Forte Band, has prominent work here, along with photographer Travis Novitsky, of the Grand Portage Band. The building itself is a work of art, sitting on the side of a rocky hill with statuesque pillars of raw pine set in the four cardinal directions; the architecture inside and out reflects the circle of life. Its galleries and exhibits feature the Ojibwe culture, the fur trade, a bookstore, multimedia programs, park offices, archives, and classrooms. The center is open year-round and is the gateway to the fort that it overlooks just below. The Heritage Center is an excellent resource for learning about a critical aspect of Minnesota's history.

Tofte

Lutsen

Grand Marais

144 miles from Duluth

58
EXIT HERE

Grand Portage National Monument
Heritage Center
Grand Portage

The Grand Portage National Monument Heritage Center houses fur trade exhibits, maintains the cultural and historical accuracy of information shared with visitors, and preserves many Native American artifacts.

Gem 59

Grand Portage National Monument

How to Get There: The Grand Portage National Monument is 39 miles north of Grand Marais. It's just past the Heritage Center on the right, on Mile Creek Road.

Accessibility: Paths are unpaved but wheelchair accessible.

Cool Things to Know: Consider this: The arrival of French explorers to this area predates the landing of the *Mayflower* at Plymouth Rock in 1620. Coming to this very spot they likely would have found the ancestors of the Grand Portage Chippewa using this fortuitous location to link their summer homes at Lake Superior to winter camps inland. Lest you think that is all in the past, know that there are still Native people in the area following in their ancestors' footsteps—tapping maple trees on the ridge above in the spring and harvesting fish from the bay below. The fort now welcomes you to take a peek into the way that life was conducted when this was the center of operations for the North West Company and the hub of the fur trade. Costumed interpreters do an excellent job sharing their knowledge and you can visit with them in the stockade, the kitchen, the great hall, and a warehouse. One of our favorites was the Historic Garden where a Three Sisters trio of corn, beans, and squash flourished. If you are feeling energetic, you might take on the Portage itself—the 8.5-mile trek from here to the remains of Fort Charlotte in the west. The trail rises some 600 feet from the shore and should give you a rough idea of what the original people and voyageurs endured to get to where they needed to go.

Tofte
Lutsen
Grand Marais
144 miles from Duluth
59 EXIT HERE
Grand Portage National Monument
Grand Portage

The fort welcomes you to take a peek into the way that life was conducted when this was the center of fur trade operations for the North West Company.

Gem 60

The Susie Islands Overlook

How to Get There: From the intersection of Highway 61 and the Grand Portage Trading Post, go 3 miles north; the Susie Islands Overlook is located just after mile marker 147. Turn right to enter the ample parking area. There are two driveways into the overlook, if you happen to miss the first one.

Accessibility: Paved and graded with curb cuts, the rest area and facilities are accessible for all.

Cool Things to Know: Panoramic best describes the views from this incredible location. Jutting out over a high cliff above Lake Superior, an observation deck gives a wide view that lets you take in all the natural and historical significance of the place.

Standing over Wauswaugoning Bay, the overlook is named for an Ojibwe word that means "where they spear fish by torchlight." Looking out, visitors can see where they sought sturgeon, whitefish, and walleye with spears in the waters below. To your left, you will see the Susie Islands off of Pigeon Point, a cluster of islands that is now uninhabited except for rare subarctic plants and water bird colonies, but once was home to an active copper mine.

Look out to sea, and if you're lucky, you can spot the tower of the Rock of Ages Lighthouse, the nearest point of the Isle Royale archipelago some 15 miles away. On a clear day you may be able to make out Isle Royale's shape, 22 miles away.

If you glance to the right from the overlook, you'll see the diabase formation known as Hat Point and its summit,

Mount Josephine, rising 750 feet above the lake. The trail to the top of Mount Josephine has spectacular views, but veteran hikers warn that it is not for the faint of heart, as it is not maintained, difficult to find, and challenging terrain.

The overlook is also known as the Wauswaugoning Bay Overlook or Mount Josephine Rest area.

The Susie Islands.

Gem 61

High Falls of Pigeon River at Grand Portage State Park

How to Get There: Proceed north on Highway 61 until you spot the U.S.-Canadian Border; just short of the border, there will be a sign indicating that a sharp left turn is required if you wish to observe the famous falls located 5.5 miles north of Grand Portage, one-half mile past Ryden's Store.

Accessibility: After approximately a half mile, the path culminates in a series of sturdy wooden boardwalks that fork at the end, providing hikers with three viewing platforms, one of which is wheelchair accessible.

Cool Things to Know: It is unlikely that you will find your journey to the High Falls to be a crowded one. When we visited the falls in late August, we saw only three other people climbing their way to the lookout. The area has a lonely and far-away feel to it; no wonder that the voyageurs considered it a rite of passage to have made the steep and arduous journey up *le grand portage*. For well over 200 years, these men of the north carried on their backs the treasures of the New World, bound for the greatest cities of Europe. Beaver pelts were nearly worth their weight in gold, and the price of a fine beaver fur hat in the first part of the 19th century was roughly equivalent to the price of a new car today. A typical voyageur was a small, compact man, not more than 5 feet, 6 inches tall. They drank and sang their way across North America, often carrying two (90-pound) packs over treacherous terrain, in this case to avoid the High Falls. So while you huff and puff your way through to the falls,

Tofte Lutsen Grand Marais Grand Portage High Falls of Pigeon River at Grand Portage State Park

imagine taking on the entire portage while carrying
180 pounds on your back, hungover and ill-fed to boot!
The falls themselves are spectacular at 120 feet and are, in
fact, the highest the state of Minnesota has to offer, though
shared as a border with Canada.

*The area has a lonely and far-away feel to it; no wonder the voyageurs
considered it a rite of passage to make the steep and arduous journey up
"le grand portage."*

About the Authors

Bill Mayo is a former Duluth resident and has lived in Two Harbors, Minnesota, since the mid 1990s. Long a part of the poetry scene of the North Shore and a former Artist-in-Residence for Isle Royale National Park, he has published work in *National Geographic Traveler, Poets Who Haven't Moved to St. Paul,* and *Zenith City Arts.* He also holds an AAS Degree in Human Services and is an enrolled member of the Leech Lake Pillager Band. His love of the North Shore came early while driving along old Highway 61 with his parents as a boy. Whether in a canoe, diving, or walking the beach, the eternal mystery of the Lake is always awe-inspiring for him.

A Minnesota native and longtime visitor to the North Shore, Kitty Mayo now resides within view of Lake Superior. Frequent trips "Up North" finally gave over to permanent residence, and Kate has drawn on her previous perspective as a visitor to the area in the compilation of these narratives. She spent most of her career in the role of counselor and is a licensed therapist and addictions counselor with an MA in counseling psychology.